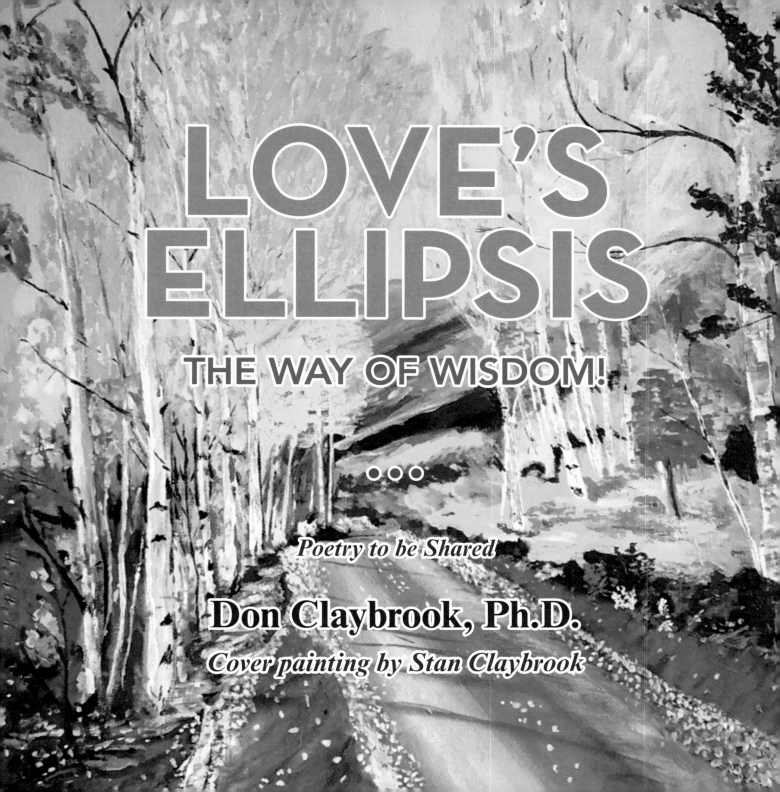

LOVE'S ELLIPSIS

THE WAY OF WISDOM!

...

Poetry to be Shared

Don Claybrook, Ph.D.

Cover painting by Stan Claybrook

AuthorHouse™
1663 Liberty Drive
Bloomington, IN 47403
www.authorhouse.com
Phone: 833-262-8899

Because of the dynamic nature of the Internet, any web addresses or links contained in this book may have changed since publication and may no longer be valid. The views expressed in this work are solely those of the author and do not necessarily reflect the views of the publisher, and the publisher hereby disclaims any responsibility for them.

Any people depicted in stock imagery provided by Getty Images are models, and such images are being used for illustrative purposes only.
Certain stock imagery © Getty Images.

This book is printed on acid-free paper.

All my Bible quotes are from the King James Version, KJV. One exception! ("Love Never Fails." The KJV says Charity never fails, an awful interpretation of the Greek translation! New International Version, NIV. The NIV is published by Zondervan in the United States and Hodder & Stoughton in the UK. The NIV was updated in 1984 and 2011.

ISBN: 978-1-6655-6441-0 (sc)
ISBN: 978-1-6655-6442-7 (e)

Library of Congress Control Number: 2022912779

Print information available on the last page.

Published by AuthorHouse 07/26/2022

authorHOUSE®

Dedication

Margaret and Stan Claybrook
Photo Credit: Paul Bright

My brother, Stan, is the artist who painted and gifted me with what has become one of my favorite painting over the years. I've used it for the cover of this book and have dubbed it, ***October Sunrise!***
Mark Twain once said of a man for whom he had very little respect, *"He was a good man in the worst sense of the word."* If you've been fortunate enough to know Stan, up close and personal, you will resonate with my assessment of my brother: Stan is a good man in the best sense of the word. To him I dedicate this book.

I also dedicate it to my three daughters, Landa Patrice, Autumn Claire and Liberty Jackson, AKA, *"Jack,"* and to my son, Don, Jr. I hope that they will see a glimpse of their dad in these poems I've written over the last 60 years. And, by association, themselves. Perhaps some words will inspire them and others will bring a smile to their faces. For sure, they will see the ridiculous. It is my hope they will also see…the profound…it's there! Oftentimes separated by only three little dots… And, I dedicate it to Lester Lee, our youngest brother, who left us all too soon…

Finally, I dedicate this book to my Lord, Jesus Christ, and ask that He use it in some small way to increase His kingdom. That's my fervent hope and prayer.

Acknowledgements

I want to thank the seven churches I've pastored down through these many years…That would be the following in chronological order: First Baptist, Redwood Valley California; First Baptist, Cloverdale California; First Baptist, Georgetown Indiana; Rolling Fields Baptist Church, Jeffersonville Indiana; South Park Baptist Church, Beaumont Texas; Mendocino Baptist, Mendocino California, and as interim pastor at Greenwood Community Church in Elk California. And finally, the Mendocino Presbyterian Church. I was never pastor there, but have served as facilitator/teacher for the co-ed adult Sunday School Class for many years.

I also want to acknowledge Cathy Allen Rowbottom, my old friend and colleague at the Mendocino Beacon and Fort Bragg Advocate-News. Before she left to run her own business as owner and operator of Fort Bragg Feed and Pet, she taught me the ropes as the Court Reporter. See the back cover for the poem she wrote for me recently. She gave me the *title-less* poem to/about, me, in jest. I gave it a title…like all the rest. ***My Replacement!***

● ● ●

Meili Daniel did the illustrations for my book, **A Kitten Named *"Little Rip!"*** Amazon, 2021. That Halloween story, inspired by events involving two of my children, Autumn Claire and Don, Jr., was 42 years in the making. I've included the very short original version which grew over the years, and used several of Meili's prints in it. I want to thank her again for a fantastic job on her first professional effort.

My Lord has blessed me with many exceptional friends. They, along with the many other friends and faithful Christians in the aforementioned churches, in addition to my own four children and four grandchildren, and my broader family, have caused me to look at life from many sides. It is my hope and prayer that this collection of 13 categories of poems is a fair and honest representation of what I've discovered

● ● ●

and what I've missed…
Don Claybrook, Sr. Ph.D. In the Year of our Lord, 2022

Preface

I've called my book of poetry, **_Love's Ellipsis_**•••**_The Way to Wisdom!_** for reasons which I hope will become apparent. I've found that the Profound in life is often separated from the Ridiculous by little more than three dots. What a statement three little dots can make!. As you read, be on the lookout for the

● ● ●

curious ellipsis! It's been used liberally in this collection of poems, and with definite intentionality!

The collection contains a little bit of everything, and a lot of something for everyone. The cover proclaims that it is _Poetry to be Shared_, and that is my intention. Please feel free to share any or all of _it (with attribution, of course)_ without asking or seeking specific or individual permission from me or my publisher. For example: I've written a Poem called _Tinker Toys and Fiddlesticks_, a tribute to both Spring Fever and my good friends, Jeannie and Brandt Stickel _(page 128)_. If you would like to send that poem to a friend, relative, enemy or otherwise, simply change the names, attribute the poem to me, then just do it. That's exactly what I did when I changed Stickel to Kellett and sent it to my good friends, Dan, Becky, and their daughter, Jordain, plus their three boys, my _"adopted"_ sons, Kieran, Cael and Jase, my _"Second Family"_ in Reno. Or, _"My First Family Not Named Claybrook."_

Table of Contents

Birth of a Masterpiece
Acrylic By Don Claybrook, Sr.

CHAPTER 1
Poems about,

The Ridiculous

AAA Tripled!

For starters, I more or less like poetry that makes a rhyme.
The snobs don't like it, but it works for me most of the time!
Now you might notice, only a few of my poems are inspired,
The rest are what some folks would say needed to be retired.

<u>But that's just poets!</u>

I for sure don't cotton to poetry when the reader has to ask,
"Wonder what the poet meant by that? What was his task?"
Usually you won't have to figure out what I'm trying to say,
Any fool can write gibberish that means nothing anyway!

<u>Any old day!</u>

Snob critiques will ask, *"What do YOU think she meant?"*
Not like I'm thinking, *"Be careful, she was heaven sent!"*
It doesn't matter what I think the fool was trying to say!
If I start fretting about all that, I'll have the *Devil to pay!*

<u>And I don't owe him a cent!</u>

Usually I have some point I want to ponder and then make.
I'm not doing brain surgery or rocket science, for gosh sake!
If I wanted to do that, I'd talk about maybe a cat with no fur,
Then rather than being a poet, I'd call myself a philosoFUR!

<u>For crying out loud!</u>

So, you see, I write poetry to entertain folks, especially me!
I'm honest! So, when I say a tree or a bee, it's a tree or a bee!
I don't try to make the tree my *thousand-year-old* Uncle!
Nor do I call a dastardly bee sting on my lip a carbuncle!

<u>It's a bee sting!</u>

I think maybe I've made my point, so I'll bring this to a close.
If you don't understand by now, you never shall, I suppose!
Thanks for listening…that is if I didn't lose you on AAA,
Some things were never meant to be. Like a pink Blue Jay!

That's all I've got to say!

Billy Bob, November 11, 2021, AKA Don Claybrook, Sr.…on my good days!

"America's Team!"

Long ago, in a faraway place, in a dark and forgotten time,
Some men got together in Dallas, writing the perfect rhyme.
Clint Murchison wanted Dallas to have an NFL football team,
Starting out awfully slowly, they would soon gather steam.

Well they had names like Dandy Don Meredith, and Bob Lilly,
And the human bullet, Bob Hayes, running cornerbacks silly.
The fastest human in history, one of the world's real scandals,
Death to defensive coordinators, pillaging them like Vandals.

Other names like Garrison, Jordan, Howley and Pearson arrived,
The Redskins played them and wondered how they could survive.
Dallas destroyed them so badly that they knew they'd been had.
The Cowboys felt like Landry, was becoming their second dad.

The league expanded and the Cowboys were placed in the NFL East,
Redskins, Giants, and Eagles were about to learn: Dallas was a beast!
Their first Super Bowl was against Johnny U. and the Baltimore Colts.
Who would soon experience the shock of lightening, with 3,000 volts.

Stats had Dallas ahead big time; but, the scoreboard would proclaim,
The Colts covered a fumble just as the 'Boys were winning the game.
Now I'm not one for complaining, if Dallas honestly flunks the test,
That day, they were the better team, ere the refs pooped in their nest.

The Cowboys would go on to win five Super Bowls, that's five of eight.
The other league teams developed against them, a most unhealthy hate.
The more Dallas won, the madder they got, the more they let off steam,
Haters hating the naming of the Cowboys, haters deciding their fate,
The 'Boys putting the blue in blue skies,
and dreaming the American Dream!
And,
Yes, we are:
America's Team!

An American Online!

The Internet, Firefox, America on-Line and Google Chrome,
I feel as if they're fiddling with me, like Nero did with Rome,
All come crashing into my mind as I try to decipher the lot,
While my ultimate demise, they clandestinely plan and plot.

Now, I couldn't see half the videos of two-thirds of my heroes.
I refuse to give into the burn. Last thing we need is two Nero's.
Not to mention the playoff games that were being shown live.
Open Settings, go to Cookies, get rid of all that shuck and jive.

Sounded good to me. I'd always loved *chocolate-chip* cookies.
One feels like a veteran trying to get along with these rookies.
But when I finally got to Settings, I couldn't find the cookie jar,
While dealing with a techie who's undoubtedly sitting in a bar.

In a language that could not be mistaken for English, he said to me,
"Dew ure bestesat to unnerstan moi." Was this a Chinese spelling bee?
"What? I thought this was an American tech, to whom I was talking.
Get me somebody I can understand, else I'm in the mood for walking."

It sounded a lot like a blue jay cussing a cat; then, the line went dead.
"Got to find some help for my computer's woes messing with my head."
Still rattled and looking for cookies, I thought, *"I'm dumb but not slow."*
I'm at my wit's end. Don't know what to do; nor, to whom I should go.
Oh wait! Boy, like I said, I'm not slow.
Bingo!
I'll Google it!

A Salty Woman!

Lot endured all the hurt that he could take.
But his wife made a fatal mistake,
And did a second-take,
When they left Sodom,

And Gomorrah.
To Lot's sorrow,
She turned to stone.
She was petrified,
And now Lot's not the only one,
Who stands alone!
But I'll throw Mrs. Lot a bone!
Perhaps as a salt-lick,
She can atone!
May 22, 2021

Boys Will Be Boys!

(Mother Brunhilda)
Mother Brun's face was like fur.
She was not cute like some nuns were.
We called her, Sir!
Like we were sons,
And nicknamed her,
Ta da!
16 Tons!
May 25, 2020

Country Music Stars!

Have you ever noticed?
Country Music stars don't age well.
All of them look like their life has gone to hell!
Hank Williams died at *twenty-nine!*
But, I guess that's better than growing old,
From chasing wild women,
And drinking cheap wine!
And singing a sad song,
With an East Texas,
<u>whine!</u>

Cowboys!

Cowboys ain't easy to love,
Even before *push-comes-to-shove!*
Heaven above,
Knows that it's true,
Like a cooing dove,
I love you!
And
The Cowboys too!
Written for Martha Lee, April 3, 2020

Don't Get Me Started With Chickens!

Getting started with backyard chickens?
Well, I'd say that's rather slim pickins.
Having led with the proverbial egg,
Leaves you eggheads up by a leg.

Now, I believe the egg was surely first,
Then, things went from bad to worse.
But if a hen started the whole thing,
It's hard to hear the evolutionary ring.
January 11, 2018

Good News/Bad News

Well, I got a piece of mail today.
Now what do they want me to pay?
The envelope said, *"Social Security."*
Gets hard to maintain one's maturity.

I opened it up with trepidation and fear.
It's almost impossible to clap and cheer.
And thought about fifty different things,
Given all the junk the mailman brings.

But wait! The first thing I saw was *"2% raise."*
So now I'll sing my government's praise.
I was so happy! I wanted to hug Uncle Sam,
While shouting *Wham, Bam, Ala Kazam!*

With such a raise I could buy more Snickers.
Must have grown weary, those old city slickers.
And a couple of more bags of Ranchers Jolly!
Praise the Lord, and *Good Golly Miss Molly!*

Oh no! My Partnership California! What about that?
My Rx will go thru the roof! The fire is out of the fat.
Because I have a low income, they cut me some slack.
And Uncle Sam will just say, *"We got your back."*

But I know better. The good news is way out of whack.
Our government simply cannot seem to stay on track
It's stupid and crazy and almost wrong, and oh so sad,
When the good news you get…is worse than the bad!
December 16, 2017

I'll wear a mask!

I'll wear a mask until the cows come home.
I'll wear a mask where the buffalos roam.
I'll wear a mask when I stand in line,
Wear it without reason or rhyme.
I'll wear one most any time.

It comes down to this: I don't want to be sick!
Even if me and that mask don't really click.
I'll wear it for Tom, I'll wear it for Dick,
But not for Harry! He's always sick.
Wear a mask! That's the trick.

I'll wear a mask whether going or coming,
I'll wear a mask while I'm humming.
I'll wear a mask even when I cry.
If you refuse, you might die.
All I need is an alibi!

I'll wear a mask when I'm singing a song,
I'll wear the blamed thing all day long.
I'll wear it when my nose is runny.
I'll wear if it's cloudy or sunny.
I'll wear it till it's not funny!

Now, if you get my drift, you better shape up,
I'll not whimper like a little whipped pup.
I'm not Dick, nor Jane, nor Sally,
Won't wear it at a Trump Rally!
Or for a Comet called Halley!

So now, let's look at the real moral of my sad tale,
Wearing masks makes us all feel like hell.
But now, if you insist on not complying,
You are selfish! And folks are dying,
What's more, I'm not buying!
September 1, 2020

I Love Sweets!

Now I love candy corn! I loved it before I was even born,
The color doesn't really matter. I'm as mad as a *Mad Hatter!*
Butterfingers are super good, wouldn't reject 'em if I could.
People know I like to gorge. I'm not as Curious as George.
The monkey!
Jolly Ranchers? Oh wow! Bring 'em all to me now!
Watermelon, wild cherry, don't forget the blueberry.
They quit making lemon, I'd eat those, even in Yemen,
I'm crazy as a pet coon, eating a 'top of a sand dune.

In the Sahara!

Well, I like each and every one, two bags and I'm done,
But watermelon's the best. Time for a JR Southfork fest.
Chocolate's as good as it gets. Give me a few more hits!
Hershey's and kisses? Neither one of those ever misses.

Much!

Then there's pecan pie, makes me want to learn to fly.
If it's served at <u>eight</u> in heaven, I'll be there at 10 to <u>seven</u>.
Walnut pie is just as good, love it in the neighborhood!
Love it to the very last nut! You think maybe I'm in a rut?

Could be!

Now licorice is pretty bad. You call that candy? How sad.
Red licorice comes in a sack, put it all on a railroad track.
Black licorice, add white, then cook it with all your might.
From the pan to the fires, you got a new set of white wall tires!

More or less.

Butterscotch has a weird taste, but don't ever let it go to waste.
Wrap it all up and send it to a Scot. He'll eat it all, on the spot.
Now any cobbler's hard to beat, causes one to become a cheat.
Apple, berry or peach, I'll eat most any cobbler within reach.

Cept Rhubarb!

I like my coffee strong and black, leave the sugar in the sack!
I don't drink it for dessert, but just to keep my mind alert.
When I drink that *foo-foo* stuff, I don't feel very tough.
Makes my mind go astray. I think that's what I drank today!

Maybe.

But pumpkin pie is awful. In many lands, it's <u>not even lawful</u>!
God made them for decor, might as well eat the outhouse door.
I cannot abide pumpkin pie. And never again am I gonna to try.
I've changed way too many diapers!
Diapers are nothing but pumpkin with windshield wipers!

Splish splash!

Bread pudding? Give me a break! One quick look's bout all I can take.
Saw mom making bread pudding once, guess she thought I was a dunce.
Add some cinnamon in it for taste, then mix it all up 'til it becomes paste.

Dirty dishwater, sugar and *day-old* bread, make folks wish they were **dead!**
I believe I've made myself clear, sugar is something that I hold dear.
Beets, brown, granulated or ribbon cane, sugar makes me go insane.
I think between that *foo-foo* coffee I consumed, and this last stanza,
You might just want to call sugar *"Don's Influanza!"*
Got it?
Unashamedly written on Wednesday, July 5, 2017
And revised in 2022

It's a Chicken-House!

Here we go again, talking about a home for a hen!
For confinement and fattening. The hen can't win.
Made of wires and bars! A real poultry refinement
Talk about hens stuck with an onerous assignment!
I think something just might be…out of alignment!
For the chickens!
Then there's a different kind of Co-op….like a mall,
It's a handy *get-together* for an economic windfall.
Everybody benefits in the co-op….Everybody wins.
Here is the best part…There's no poop in the coop.
Tell that to the hens!
Then there's a two-door car, a coupe….or a *coupé.*
In French, unlike coop, it sounds more like *toupée*!
But it rhymes with where the chickens go to poop,
At least in English it does….. Well that's the scoop!
But don't tell the chickens!
An artificial hairpiece worn to cover a bald spot.
A coop, co-op, *coupé* or coupe*,* a *toupée* is not!
So when it comes to chicks….just call me an ally!
I guess I'm a fan of the chicken; or, at least I try!
Do you suppose the chickens even care?
Well, I hope they do; but, I cannot lie!
If I don't give them a boost,
They'll still get by!

And come home
To roost.
By and
<u>Bye.</u>

It's a Hoax!

I know that elephants don't fly,
It's just another *pie-in-the-sky,*
But me oh my,
If this is true,
Tis,
Another reason,
I vote blue!
July 15, 2020

It's Up to You!

Somebody told me that rhyming lines doesn't a poem make;
So, I thought I would engage in a little bit of *give and _ _ _ _.*
I'm not saying they're wrong; and, I'm not saying they're right,
Just that some things simply follow, *like day follows _ _ _ _ _.*
I went to see my doctor with symptoms of *poems that rhyme.*
And she told me that good health depended on a *stitch in _ _ _ _.*
Then I asked her, *"What's that got to do with why I live in a fog?"*
She looked at me like she'd been bitten by *a junk yard _ _ _.*

So, I thought, *"Where do I go now?"* Ah, my pastor, he should know.
It would have been better if I'd watched a whale's blowhole _ _ _ _.
Something along the lines of biblical advice, like the Golden Rule,
Like the song by Chuck Berry, *Up in the morning and off to _ _ _ _ _ _.*

Now, I suppose the moral of this sad tale goes something like this:
Rhyming lines is death's notice that comes with a well-placed _ _ _ _.
On the other cheek of course, without passion or too much emotion.

And with no more tears than it would take to fill-up the Pacific _ _ _ _ _.
Now if this bunch of nonsense is viewed as *a dog that won't hunt*,
Perhaps my doggerel verse is not a strikeout; but, neither is it a _ _ _ _.
And really, it doesn't rhyme at all, that is, unless you read it that way,
When all is said and done, perhaps you've made more to be done,
Than what I've had to _ _ _.
May 1, 2018

Lofty Aspirations!

Finding a chicken's gizzard,
Or a snowball in a blizzard,
Takes a Wizard!
Now here's my goal:
To
Find a lizard, with a soul!
*
Guess you think I'm on a roll,
But being a poet,
Takes its toll.
January 18, 2020

Lyrics for Life!

Old Willie sings *"Just turn out the lights, the party's over."*
But some of us are pleased as punch, thanks to Russell Stover!
The rest of us are just waiting, biding our own sweet time.
Will a dollar never be worth more than a Continental dime?

Mr. Davis, Louisiana's governor, sang, *"You Are My Sunshine."*
While Mr. John Muir, wrote about a lonesome Ponderosa Pine!
I doubt if either one of these gents was having very much fun.
Like Roger Miller, picking guitar by ear, and nose with his gun.

Kenny taught us just to hold 'em or fold 'em, while playing cards,
But he didn't tell us that we'd likely be playing with prison guards.
Tom Jones yearned to go to the *"Green, green grass of home."*
And Leo Tolstoy taught us how to recognize and shun a tome!

John D. Rockefeller showed us how to make a million bucks,
And NASCAR taught us how to drive cars and jacked up trucks.
Countless others have taught us how to mend broken hearts,
Precious few have instructed us on how to pick up the parts.

Dorothy taught us something better's just beyond our rainbows,
And Jesus taught it's rarely best to walk the way the wind blows.
Eddy sang, *"I'll hold you in my heart till I can hold you in my arms,"*
Rockwell's paintings? From freckled-faced boys to Gothic charms.

Well now, there's lots of other songs I could write about,
Like Chubby Checkers belting out, *"Twist and Shout!"*
But then again, I think I'll bring this mess to an abrupt end,
By simply saying, "I'm sorry y'all, it's too late to amend!"
I guess you could sing, *"It's a sin."*
Or,
You win Again!
June 20, 2019

March and Masks!

March! Ringing a hint of Spring's bells.
February's dead and already smells,
As winter pales.
So ditch those masks,
Because hope prevails!
That's our task.
Happy Trails!
(If we don't first,go off the rails!)
March 1, 2022

Motionless!

When President Coolidge died,
Not very many people cried!
Nobody tried.
That rings a bell,
Then,
Some wag cried,
"But how can you tell?"
March 27, 2021

My Big Sis!

(Lanora)
This was her doppelganger:
*Dean Sourpuss Priss Alec…*with some anger.
Played her fanger,
Sewing her clothes,
On Mom's Sanger,
With her nose!
April 11, 2019

My Day in Court!

Judge in black, lawyers in blue,
I'm in back, without a clue.
Back in trouble, out on a limb,
Could be my double, sink or swim.

Neck in a noose, mind in a mess,
Hanging loose, wearing a dress.
Defendants jumping, gender in doubt.
DA's humping, heavyweight bout.

Orange jump-suits, sentence in tow.
Five O'clock shadow, watching it grow.

Public Defender, is doing his best,
To free an offender, who's just confessed.

Bench warrants and motions, truths and lies,
Land O' Goshen, and apple pies.
All sorts of cases, big and small,
A day at the races, a *"cattle-call."*

Custody calendar, twist and shout.
Flying fur, the cons want out.
Don't understand, what makes 'em tic.
Sometimes bland, sometimes slick.

Raise your hand, get sworn in.
Contraband! Now that's a sin.
Makes you think, right is wrong.
Wanting to drink, a cheating song.

Court is done, count the cost.
Little is won, much is lost.
I want to nod, I want to cry.
But for the grace of God, there go I.
When I was a Newspaper Court Reporter, 2001-2014
Dedicated to my friend, Tim Stoen, Deputy District Attorney
For the Mendocino Coast at Ten Mile Court!

My Favorite Recipe!

Making a recipe from scratch,
Makes me itch when I try a batch!
But it's met its match,
And it should,
When down the hatch
It tastes good.
But,

I knew it would!
June 9, 2021

Odds and In's!

Roosters and hens, and double chins,
And all those *"What-might-have-beens!"*
Just add my sins.
Then I'll implore,
Am I out or in?
What's in store?
But wait!
Who's keeping score?
If I'M
not in…my friend,
Then you don't have a chance!
So, It looks like you,
Just missed the dance!
August 4, 2021

Ode to A Plumber!
(The sorriest story ever told)

They say that old plumbers never die…they just fade away.
Cold, wet, and hoping to dry, and live to plumb another day.
Now here's an ode to that fair trade, I've lived it; so, I know,
Just plumb your mind and plumb those depths, any way to
"Make a show."
A wrenched back, a tempted soul, growing old way too soon.
Digging in dirt like a mole, *roughing-in* houses by the moon.
Parts are scarce and time short, and the pot's lost all its lead,
When you think you're just about dead. a familiar voice yells,
"Just use your head!"
By *"parts"* I'm talking baling wire, blocks and pieces of stone.
And, when straits are dire, you work your fingers to the bone.

After the day is done, and you're too tired for hopes or wishes,
At that very moment in time, we'd hear those magical words,
"The girls will do the dishes!"
Here's a nice afterthought, as this sad ode comes to a screech.
The Lord was being kind…when He called _this_ plumber to preach.
Enough of this, I've had my say. Life's tough. It's hard. It's cold.
Truth is…at end of day, plumbing's the sorriest story ever told.
☺Except for washing those dishes☺
That's still one of my wishes

**Our Old Milk Cow!**
(The Dow-Jones Report!)

Jack! Why don't you try to make yourself useful around here?
What was that? I guess I could stand and cheer, *Daddy Dear!*
You could start by milking that old cow! When??? Like now!
If you'd show me how, I'd milk the cow like Jones does Dow!
Oh, Wow!
If I remember correctly, that duo lists averages and quotes!
It's all about as useless as castles without surrounding moats!
You remember hearing this? *The Dow's up! The Dow's Down!*
Or Miss Amelia Earhart taking a break in *Lost and Found?*
That's not sound!
You gonna help around here, or make unpleasable blurbs?
If I can't disturb liquid nouns and make squeezable verbs,
Who's going to milk our Holstein which you call, *Luvabull?*
The milk will never get to the pail! It'll stay up *above-able.*
In *Miss Luvabull!*
Well, just you never mind. I'll do it my own self.
While you're putting your trophies on the shelf,
You can find other weird ways to be useful.
Just from being callow and youthful!
Now is that,
A lot of bull?
or
Truthful?

17

Poem For Zeke (at his request!)

I promise not to write a poem about it,
Surely don't want to get you in an all-out snit!
So, I'll just leave it as it is,
Otherwise, it's nobody's biz!
Oh, I know! Snit's are one of your favorite things,
Because you enjoy how that bell rings!
But, I'll just resist and leave it alone,
To do it, would be like given a mad dog a bone.
Merry Christmas, Zeke,
And don't forget the ***Reason For The Season!***
(for much the same reason as I sign my name in Blue.
And that would be,
Dr. Don…to you!
P.S. I'd rather be dead…than sign it in **Red!**
December 23, 2021

Porta-Potty Party-Time!

Well now, I'm just not going to take it, very much more.
No more gazing at the walls…no more walking the floor.
I'm just weary of being alone…inside these prison walls,
Just too many bad memories; and, other such sad recalls.

The only time I really talk is when I'm watching bad T. V.
Or when I'm just gazing at videos…which I can hardly see.
But, I'll talk to either one of them…when sacred duty calls.
Only assignment worse than this? Visiting shopping malls!

Now where one's heart is, they say, that will also be home.
The heart warmly lodges there…just as bubbles do in foam.
But, I awaken every morning…with an urgent need to go.
Don't know what I'm talking about? You <u>really are</u> slow!

The fact you're still reading this poem, is really just enough.
Proves you have little to do. Would you like a dip of snuff?
Other stunts are candidates… if one has nothing else to do,
Crying-out-loud or writing bad poetry… just to name two.
Now where do ya think I'm going, with this mess of mine?
Think maybe I'm gargling, with something like turpentine?
Well, you ain't far off. I'm going to put a Porta-Potty, I think,
In the middle of our parking lot… just to make a stink.

Now, when I'm bored to tears, you know exactly what I'm gonna do.
I'm going to write awful, doggerel poetry…. and blame it all on you.
Now, that will make your day!
And my day too!
Monday, July 3, 2017

Rain!

Rain is so refreshing, *life-giving* and wet,
With problems we often want to forget.
A blessed trinity that's *two-thirds* great;
Staying dry's in our DNA! A *built-in* fate.

But, we thank you Lord when the rains come,
At least it puts an end to the *ho-hum-drum!*
But,
Could you space them out just a wee bit more?
The threshold's so wet, I can't close my door!

Lord, you know that I keep my word…mostly,
Though in so doing, I wax somewhat verbosely,
While doing my best to stay true to myself,
You end up putting me down low on a shelf.

Don't get me wrong, I know that rain is a gift.
Perhaps Lord, you're sifting me through a sift.
Trying me to see if I'll pass Your Ultimate Test.

Don't worry Lord, this doggerel is all in jest!
But, **YOU** already knew that! I guess.
December 17, 2018

The English Language!

What a mess! One fish is just a fish,
And yet, two or more of them are still fish.
Why don't they get their act together?
Like birds of the proverbial feather?
O well, I guess we can always wish,
If the English language is to weather.
I suppose if I were to get my wishes,
I'd do what the King James Bible does,
When it calls more than one fish, fishes,
But it's likely to call were, was!
And sometimes for "Biz," it say, "Buzz!"
And has Abraham calling Sarah,
His "Cuz."
May 29, 2021

The Geriatric Shuffle!

I'm getting old, but I still get around like a young man.
From Fort Bragg, Stockton and Elk; but, not Pakistan,
And I get up and go where the sky and roads take me.
From Louisville to Laredo, Wounded Knee to Waikiki.

Corpus Christi, Lodi, San Antonio, Reno; but not Siam,
Waco, Mendocino, Flour Bluff have made me who I am.
Yon Sydney, the Great Barrier Reef and Mineral Wells,
And so many more of life's hills, rivers and happy trails.

Spent a spell in Beaumont, Texas in The Golden Triangle,
Which all ended when my life became a hopeless fandangle.

Higher Education was in the textbooks for my middle two.
Upon arrival, I was beset by myriad choices. So, who knew?

And also, there's London, Paris, St. Petersburg and Madrid,
Wanted to do China, but the SARS epidemic soon got unhid.
And the White Cliffs of Dover; yet, I've never been to Nome.
I got my China rebate and it was good just to stay at home.

South America was wonderful! We did the ABC's. That trio,
Would be Argentina and Brazil, with Buenos Aires and Rio.
Ipanema and Copacabana were nice, but so was old Chile.
And the ubiquitous, but always delightful, *Hard Rock Café.*

Nor to Antarctica, land of the frozen tundra and polar bear.
 Like, *"Why didn't you Just say, 'I've been everywhere.'"*
That kind of barren wasteland is bound to simply amaze ya.
 Good question; but, truth be told, I've never been to Asia.

I came so close when we were in Chile and Punto Arenas,
 Down south and a few miles straight down from Uranus.
Down very near to Cape Horn and *the jumping-off -place.*
 But, I was bound for Santiago, with a smile on my face.

Africa's quite likely my favorite to endure the test of time,
Sweetwater was sweet with its sugary namesake sublime.
Nairobi was a modern makeover of an old ancient tribe.
Missionaries, safaris and crocks. Catch the nascent vibe?

I've taken you on this grand tour with me in order to say,
 "Don't fool yourself thinking I've turned a new leaf today,
Slowing down, relaxing, and getting my feathers in a'ruffle,"
I never intended to get so old, as to do the *Geriatric Shuffle!*
May 8, 2018,

The Greatest Poem Never Written!

As I sit here at my keyboard reflecting on various and sundry things,
Parked here in my swivel chair, to see what quiet inspiration brings,
My mind dreams of doing something that'll be the best concept ever.
I don't want to delay until some fool says, *"Better late than never!"*
Oh wait,
I've got it! I'll do it! Here it is; I'll write the best poem known to man!
Shakespeare might mess his grave, but he'll be a full-blown dead fan.
The world will throw me a parade and give me the Nobel Peace Prize!
I'll go to work on a draft, then sit back and see what will materialize.
So now,
I can hardly wait to get started! The world lingers with bated breath.
They'll probably want to give me a <u>*nom de plume*</u>, maybe *Dr. Death*!
I'll knock their sox off and give them a nice classic poem for the ages,
That'll be after I kill 'em dead with these incredible verses and pages.
And,
So now it's four hours later, and my back is beginning to hurt a lot.
A glance at the monitor and I see I've written neither spurt nor spot.
This day's halfway gone and I've given my gray matter time to work.
I can write the best poem ever; or else I can start the coffee to perk.
However,
I'm set on writing this poem, if I can just come up with a clever plan.
But my brain must be 'bout the size of a marble, in *Never-Never Land*.
Now I'm starting to think that *world-class* inspiration is like a vapor,
And, I'll never write a classic, if I don't put something on this paper.
But stop!
Making History will just have to wait, because genius takes it's time.
Five will get you ten by then, I'll have neither a reason nor a rhyme.
I'll work on this world renowned, incredible poem again next week.
Like the Bible says, *"You will never find it, unless you start to seek!"*
Seeking might just be a better plan when the genius is feeling meek!
April 25, 2019

The Second Shot!

Who needs a grove of those *brown-robed* Druids,
When you've got Autumn Claire and Martha Lee?
Autumn C. said that my body needed lots of fluids,
Martha Lee said it was liquids…They don't agree.

Well the only fluid I ever heard of was for brakes,
Liquid nitrogen is the propellant that's in rockets.
It wouldn't take this old cowboy too many takes,
To comprehend he'd be hurting in all his sockets.

I'll go with the brake fluid, It's better than bleach!
Nitro would cause a pretty loud explosion, a POP!
They keep it under lock and key, and out of reach,
With brake fluid, I won't get hooked, because I can
Always

March 13, 2021, upon getting sick from the 2nd Moderna shot.

The Tooth Fairy!
Did You Ever Eat Paste?

Oh, the lengths to which I'll go,
Just to touch base…with people I know!
But then again, all I had to do,
Was *cut-and-paste* a time or two,
From my Diary/Journal!
*
Some things would just go to waste,
If it weren't for *cut-and-paste!*
But,

The only thing wrong with eating paste…
Was the taste!
That's what made me chaste!
Ooops! I'd best make haste,
Or stop eating paste!
I didn't want this report to go to waste!

When I lost my first tooth, I was paid a dime…By the Tooth Fairy! That's why I still check under my pillow each morning! And that old wolf's skull I found, on the other side of the railroad tracks there in Graham Texas? Well, it was so old that there wasn't much left of it except a mouth full of big teeth. And they didn't pay one cotton picking penny, even though I left them under my pillow for three nights.
Moral of this sad tale? You can't fool the Tooth Fairy…or your mother!
February 17, 2022

"The Weatherman!"

Well the forecast is for scattered showers.
Tomorrow's mud is April's flowers,
And May's bowers,
Nevertheless, The weather sours,
Lots of disarrays!
However, forecasting pays.
But, for crying out loud!
They can't even guess,
Yesterday's!

This is Your Captain, Charlie Brown!

Sit back, relax, we'll get you there on time,
And you'll give me a dollar for my worthless dime.
We'll fly this baby like a *super-sonic* kite.
Or maybe we won't; but, again, maybe we might.

We'll zip from LAX to SFO and then on to STS,
Before this day is done, I'll be damning this airport mess.

That's *Santa Rosa-Sonoma* for folks in the *no-flight* zone,
Just Charlie Brown and Lucy, giving Snoopy his bone.

I don't put much stock in hijackers and such.
That would stretch my imagination a bit too much.
But this guy sitting beside me with a towel on his head,
Makes me think before this day is done, I might be dead.

Turns out his name is Maurice; but a Muslim to be sure.
Then I learn that he's a Christian, good, straight and pure.
One never knows until he flies out of Charlie Brown,
That it's safer than his place on the ground.
January 2, 2018

Those Were the Days!
(My family)

Will somebody bring me a fruit jar;
Or maybe a nice big vessel to pee in?
Hurry up, I can't even walk very far.
I guess I'll just bear it all with grin.

I didn't sleep much at all last night,
I went pert near completely blind!
Wouldn't nobody turn on the light.
I couldn't see to wipe my behind.

Bring me something for my burn,
I bout singed all my hair by half.
Nobody thought it was their turn.
Hurts real bad! Don't even laugh.

What's for supper? I'm starving, Ruth!
My stomach thinks my throats been cut.
Now I'm telling God's absolute truth,

I need some ointment put on my butt.
Whose water is this in the wash basin?
I need to use it to wash up my face.
I'm sweaty from working and pacing,
Will somebody just *cut to the chase?*

Tell Les to turn up the TV on the shelf!
I don't think I can get up off this couch.
"For Pete's sake Henry, I'll do it myself!"
Thanks Ruth! Now get me my pouch.

So, they had six kids, reared 'em all,
And got one and all a good education.
The boys wrestled and played football,
Because of them. We had a vacation!

It's Stan, Don, Lala, Lib, Dot and Les,
Three boys and three girls, they were.
Henry and Ruth created quite a mess,
But it was all *"yes ma'am! Yes sir!"*

The years passed by, the kids did too,
The times they were a 'changing fast.
The skies were not always very blue,
And the good times? They never last.

Now, as I look back over the years,
And ponder all that I've said above,
I thank my Lord with joyful tears,
It all worked out,
In spite of our fears,
Like white on a dove,
Because,
We had love!
April 24, 2019

Twenty Ways to the Happy Life?

If you wanna be happy, wear the best and prettiest shoes,
While the other five *"You's"* world-wide, give you the blues.
And so, if you just sit on your butt eleven hours every day?
And sleep without a pillow, you've got the devil to pay?
So, I hear you talking. My dad was tall and my mom was fat.
And I'll be able to resist women, food, danger, and all that?
And if I shake my head real hard, my limbs will come to life?
And if I chew all my food on the right, that will end all strife?

Tea bags in my stinking tennis shoes? Takes me back to # one.
And going without sleep eleven hours a day, well, I'd be done.
If I'm not mistaken, Einstein is right. In four years I'd unfurl.
Even if I eat all them red, green and gold apples in the world,

Which comes first the chicken or the egg, healthy or laughing?
And Wikipedia wanting to cut your life in two by just halving?
And being lazy and inactive might kill you quicker'n smoking,
A ten-watt light bulb's got gonna help you? You gotta be joking?

When taking a bath, my body temp don't heat the water one bit.
But could eat razor blades when stomach acid is pitching a fit.
And, about that ovum being big'ern a sperm by a country mile?
No thank you, I'll just keep on living with a big ole Texas smile.
March 7, 2018

Weather Report!

At 8:04 a.m. by the clock,
Here are the temps in a diagonal block;
54/59; That's a high of fifty-nine;
Partial clouds, but looking fine;
Moderate AQ at 52;
Wind WSW at 2, too;

Pressure is 30 ought seven;
Visibility 5 miles, but I can still see heaven!
So, I'll take the day just as God sends it;
With the notable exception of how man rends it.
Now, that's your coastal weather report,
And the last thing I need this morning,
Is a Texas, *smart-mouth* retort!
Of any sort!
August 14, 2021

When Things Go South!

"You're a dish!! I'm fond of you."
She heard, *"I wish you a *mond adeau."*
Now here's a clue!
Bottom line, friend.
Neither one'll do.
You can't win!
*Mond, a variation of mound (big!)

Who Put the Boo in the Bouffant?

Who, who, who put the boo, boo, boo in the Bouffant?
She was Austin's grandmother…gurgling like a gurgling font.
A hairdo sweeping the country in the *mid-80's* to *mid-90's,*
Every gal had to have one, be their stature *super-size* or tiny's.
Or perhaps trying to distract from their larger than life hineys?
However,
I should have said, Martha was holding Baby Austin in this shot!
Whether he's been bathing and Martha took him out, I know not.
I'd cautioned her, *"Don't throw the baby out with the bathwater."*
In the photo I saw, he looked not unlike a drowning sea otter!
But,
I might have been interpreting it like a Rorschach *ink-blotter.*
Now, I digress! What really mattered is she looked like <u>*Miss Texas!*</u>

Driving half the men in Texas *half-wild,* giving the other *half-hexes.*
For all of them fell in love with her from going *"about half-way-wild"*
I think I understand her secret. Had to be that bouffant hairstyle!
Martha Lee *Put The Boo, in The Bouffant,* by a country mile!
March 17, 2021

Xylophoning!

(Don, the Percussionist)
If I were in the twilight zone,
I'd get myself a Xylophone,
And one,
With a half bad tone.
Because,
I'm a bad dude!
And,
I'd whack that bone,
With attitude!
May 28, 2019

Thanks for putting up with my nonsense, i.e; **The Ridiculous!** However, Behavioralists say that one of the most telling characteristics which shows if someone is unusually intelligent, is a well-developed sense of humor. If you made it this far in my book of poetry, chances are you're likely way above average in I.Q. If you didn't read this page, someone who did, should tell you not to fret. I.Q. is likely given at birth in one's DNA; and, it's not your fault at all! Or as the legendary University of Texas Longhorns football coach, Darrell Royal, once suggested, *"You got to dance with the one who brung you!"*

Which just might be one reason that Southern Baptist eschew dancing! On the other hand, I'm now a *Baptistaterian;* so, that solves the dancing conundrum. However, if the Holy Spirit decided to move in a mighty way at 12:00 noon on Sunday, and in the Presbyterian Church, and the preacher went to 12:15 p.m., because of the Spirit's movement, it would only upset the people because they didn't get out at 12:00 noon precisely! The Scripture tells us, *"The Spirit moves where He wills."* Now that also implies *"when"* He wills.

And, if you don't agree with it, well there ya go...right out the door, on your way to something else you cannot wait to leave. Preachers know this kind of stuff...in both churches! Don't ever get Sister Soulsaint on your case for causing her to burn the casserole she has in her oven with the timer set for 11:38 a.m. Hell hath no fury like a Saint with a burned casserole!

Should anyone find that anything I've had to say in any of these 337 poems which has helped you, please send me an email and tell me about it. I would consider that a blessing. My email address is the very last thing I've written, and on the last page of this book.

Speak Softly But Carry a Big Stick
Don Claybrook, Sr. Photo credit, Don Claybrook, Jr.

CHAPTER 2
Poems about,

TIME

Heraclitus' River!

Heraclitus said, *"You can never cross the same river twice."*
The river's geography remains, but the river is not the same!
Steinbeck said, *"It's kind of like comparing men with mice."*
Both DNA's intuiting that survival's the name of the game,
With neither showing shame!
Teddy Roosevelt said, ***"Speak softly, but carry a big stick!"***
And showed what he meant in his charge up San Juan Hill
Watergate gave us novel TV, and the demise of *Tricky Dick!*
And taught us that *"Plumbers"* can handle a *break-in thrill,*
On a different kind of hill!
So, it seems that Mr. Heraclitus' point was rather profound.
When our eyes and minds are opened upon further inspection.
Then we've discovered the truth which that sage had found,
Yesterday river is *parti pour toujours,* the French connection!
Upon reflection,
As all rivers are inevitably so bound,
Now…that's profound!
*
December 16, 2021

A Moment in Time!

June was just a moment in time.
Went away like a church chime!
Died in it's prime!
But I must confess,
It was sublime,
Nontheless.
June 30, 2021

A New Twenty-Four!

Thank you, Father, for a brand new day.
And for giving me life…another *twenty-four*.
Will I spend it, walking in *"The Way?"*
Or simply whiling it away…walking the floor?

My heart says that I must reject the latter,
While faithfully accepting the former.
And walk in the light of things that matter,
Not perfectly hot, but somewhat warmer.

That's certainly not to say I won't sin at all.
No, history says, that would not be my style,
While thinking I might stand, I'm sure to fall.
Missing His perfect will, by a country mile!

Now that's my dilemma, as I think on what to do.
Shall I read the Word; or, should I watch TV?
Whatsoever things are good, right, lovely and true,
May not be the answer, but they surely hold the key.

So, after much, much thought, and a little prayer,
I've chosen in favor of TV. That's my decision.
And I think my choice not wrong, but right and fair,
Though, it will be met with lots of hate and derision.

I've accepted my Lord's call to the abundant life!
And thrown all caution away…Gone with the wind.
Fighting *"yes"* or *"No"* leads to bitterness and strife.
Problems with that? Perhaps you need to learn to bend.

Lord, I close this verse with this tentative thought.
It seems you've turned my *naught* to *ought!*
Thank you Father, for a new *twenty-four!*
And…for my forevermore!

Your loving kindness,
Sweeps me away.
What more can I say?
I'll go on loving you,
Come what may!
August 26, 2019

April!

April drives me insane,
As March's madness goes down the drain.
This sad refrain,
Will it ever end?
Then shouts my brain,
"Don't Break!
Bend!"
April 1, 2019

April in Paradise!

April's here! It's no mystery.
It's arrived on this day for much of history!
So shed no tears.
April we'll eulogize.
March is clear,
Because,
We also
Euthanize!
This ain't Paradise! By any measure.
You're welcome. It's my *"PLEASURE"*
If not my treasure!!
April 1, 2021

At The End of The Day!

So, at the end of the day,
Hell, high water or come what may.
Home or away!
Some sage will bark,
"At the end of the day,
It gets dark!"
January 19, 2020

August Nights!

Hot August nights, yes indeed!
Make this old man go to seed.
But all I need,
Is my Lord above,
A _"can-do"_ creed,
And a woman's love.
August 1, 2019

Blue Monday!

It's Blue Monday. How do I know?
Well, I don't need a calendar to tell me so!
I do have a soul though.
So, who put the hue in blue?
Or the colors in the rainbow?
I know it wasn't you!
And I'm way too slow,
I haven't a clue.
So before we let this Blue Monday go,
Let's give God His due.
I will. Will you?
March 24, 2021

Changing Times!

Well now, they're messing with my mind again!
Cause the guy on TV was barking like *Rin-Tin-Tin!*
So I picked up my remote to turn the volume louder,
But *Old Kibbles and Bits* took an extended powder.

When he who'd taken a leave of absence came back,
I was all set for anything, even expected some flack.
Like the *Wizard of Oz*, I could only hear his voice,
But by then I was rapt, didn't think I had any choice.
And here's what he said:
"At 2 A.M. turn your clocks back one hour!"
But,
Said that in Spring too! This time I wasn't gonna cower,
Because in the Spring change I saw no reason or rhyme,
And so I wasn't going to fall for that con again this time.

Well, to make a long story short…and it's too late for that.
So I'll just cut to the chase and deal with this fire in the fat.
In Spring I slept through the *spring-forward change-tier,*
And,
Was stuck with 19 clocks an hour off, the whole darn year!
However,
This time I've got a plan to circumvent all that nonsense.
Might say that I'm looking for some kind of recompence.
Now don't you tell anybody what I've got up my sleeve,
But this changing of time is my number one *pet peeve.*

What will I do? I'm gonna change all 19 of my clocks,
And you might think I'm nothing more than a sly old fox.
But,
Rather than set my alarm to get up and change them at 2,
Here's exactly what I plan to do,
I'll change them all before I go to bed, and do it on the sly,
Without even having to tell them, one cotton picking lie!
November 7, 2021

Day-Tripping!

Benbow Inn and breakfast too,
Avenue of the Giants, these precious few!
Will dreams come true,
With this request?
Just say, *"We do,"*
And be my guest.

February!

A month with twenty-eight days,
Which in each fourth year changes ways.
A *Leap-Year* phase,
February's mess,
Twenty-nine days,
Or less!
February 1, 2019

February 2021!

Well, some say the rain falls on the unjust, as well as on the just!
While others contend that, *"Promises were made to be broken."*
Winter and Spring rains and promises might settle the dust,
And many of our reckless thoughts may be left unspoken.
But till pie crusts and nails turn into crumbs and rust,
And all our promises become more than just a token,
We will go from *The Big Bang* to *The Big Bust,*
Until all of our better angels are woken!
And in Him, we once again Trust!
And that's not an option!
IT'S A MUST!
February 1, 2021

Flowing to Saturday!

Saturday is the last day,
Even though it's before Sunday.
That's just the way,
Weeks seem to flow.
And,
All this to say,
"There you go!"
May 23, 2020

Friday's Alure!

Penultimate Fridays bring,
Hope for weekends and a nice Spring.
That has a ring!
What's the cure?
A Bluebonnet fling!
And that Texas allure!
May 24, 2019

Fridays Are Good!

I love Fridays, that's for sure!
Might be the day we find a cure.
What's
COVID'S allure?
It's way past due.
Simple and pure?
Now,
There's a clue!
May 22, 2020

Friday Forevermore!

T'was a day I can't ignore,
That Friday she slipped out my door.
I walk the floor,
From dusk to dawn,
But forevermore,
She'll be gone.
May 24, 2019

Good Morning October!

Good Morning, from me to you!
The sky's still blue,
And so are my eyes,
But that's no surprise,
So, let's analyze!
This October surprise!
With a bit of red,
Thrown in too!
No Dummy, not the month…the EYES!
But that's not the surprise!
And I'll tell you no lies?
The problem is,
ONE TOO MANY TRIES!
Oct. 1, 2021

Hello 2021!

COVID came! Our world was rent,
But His Love is always toward us bent,
Grace heaven sent,
And
Always plenty!
What up and went?
2020!
New Year's Day, 2021

High School Days!

Halcyon days and high schools,
The girls were hip and the guys were fools.
But all kept their cools.
Nevertheless,
Those days are gone,
As if they were never!
Time does have rules,
They sever!
But we *remember,*
Those days,
<u>Forever!</u>

I found a Dime Today!

If seeing is believing,
And space is really time,
Then wanting is achieving,
And poetry's more than rhyme.
If life is really about more money,
The currency of space and time,
Then I'm an overachiever.
Today, I found a dime!
At a special place
In time.
Summer 1992

January!

Well, the old year has parted,
Dare not face the new, *half-hearted.*
Time's aborted!
But won't stand still.
So

Let's get started,
Shuffle or deal!
January 1, 2019

January 2021!

Twenty-twenty! What a shame!
Still, I heard that Santa Clause came!
But, COVID's no game,
That's plain to see.
So, who's to blame?
You or me?
Well now,
That _blame-game's_ about halfway lame!
It just might be…Bobbie McGee?
But hey! Whats in a name?
It could be all three!
So, if it's a game,
Tic-tac-toe,
Who's got the key
?
Now that's so lame.
But here's what I see.
It's all three!
January 1, 2021

July!

Mid-year sunshine. It's July!
Makes a grown man want to cry.
Well, me oh my,
If it's not hot,
Then truth's a lie,
And Santa's not!
May, 2019

June!

June is lovely, nice to endure,
half a year waxing more mature.
The days are pure,
As winter's snow,
The nights as sure,
As Yes and No!
June 1, 2019

June! May's Last Tune!

It was inevitable that May give way to June,
Just as the tide cedes control to the moon,
Or puts the hue in a blue lagoon.
But why did June sneak in at midnight?
Do we just whistle May's Last Tune,
Without a fight?
It came way too soon!
But like I say,
Both day and night,
Whatever's right!
June 1, 2021

Lost Forever!

Some years are lost forever,
Which we simply have to sever.
They were never,
Meant to stay
Just an endeavor
Gone astray.

March!

March is a month that shouts, *"Spring!"*
Wildflowers do their own sweet thing,
Where colors cling,
And blend their hues,
And lovers sing,
Their,
"I love yous."
March 1, 2019

March Madness X!
(Cat's Paws)

Is March nothing more than a sad refrain?
A tedious repeat of last month's rain,
Going insane, or feeling no pain?
But hey! Wait a minute!
Hold on there.
Ok?
Let's just,
Tarry a hair,
And think a bit.
Life with no pain,
Has very little whiz,
There's not much to gain.
For where there's no foam,
There is scarcely, if any, fizz!
Foam follows fizz like effect does cause,
And,
Love follows the heart, like a cat does its paws!
Well,
There it is. I'm done. Happy March, Twenty twenty-one.
March 1, 2021

May!

Slotted between April and June,
May's tides are controlled by the moon,
But none too soon,
The days turn warm,
and
While lovers swoon,
Honeybees swarm.
May 1, 2019

May, 2021!

The other day I exclaimed, *"May!"*
Whatever happened to yesterday?
And the dragons I was about to slay?
Are we already five months in?
Old Man Time, what do you say?
You're hard to keep at bay.
So well,
Let's all go play!

Mondays!

Now, some say that Mondays are blue.
That just might be, I've had a few.
My time is due,
To be alone.
I'll face that too.
So,
Bring it on!
May 27, 2019

My Sad Day!

My gosh, what a day it was,
With naught up, not even a buzz.
When doesn't, does,
Is distant kin,
And a kissing Cuz,
A *"has been!"*
July 22, 2019

1956!

Nineteen-fifty-six came.
Korea was a distant flame.
All shared the blame.
Ugly to the bone,
Some dead…all lame!
Life goes on!

1957!

Times were like springtime always.
Nineteen-fifty-seven days,
Life's purple haze,
With very few fears.
Halcyon days,
We,
Shed no tears!

1957 Days!

Nineteen-fifty-seven days,
All wrapped up in a golden haze.
The latest phase,
Those times we stole,
The newest craze,
<u>To unfold.</u>

November!

November! The nights grow long,
Leaving me with a sad old song.
But what could go wrong,
In time and space,
Now that I bask,
In His embrace!
November 1, 2019

October!

What's the October surprise?
Well now,
There are no more tears in my eyes!
Only blue skies,
And sparkling nights!
And this implies,
Wrongs,
Become rights.
October 1, 2019

October Surprise!

I have no notion just when,
We will then all wake up again.

But it's no sin,
To be sober,
The first day in,
October!
Oct. 1, 2021

Penultimate Thursday!

Some days barely make the cut.
Thursday is the penultimate,
I confess!
Nevertheless,
Out of that rut,
Weekends abut,
May 21, 2020

Potpourri of Spring!

Mopping and dusting and vacuuming too,
Raking fallen leaves and mowing to do.
Calendars to plan and nights to sleep,
Daydreams to dream and promises to keep.

Why don't you diet? You have no control!
Why don't you *"get down?"* You have no soul.
Why don't you eat? You're looking so thin,
Why aren't you happy? Why can't you bend?

Promises and daydreams, both can be broken,
Good words and bad words, both can be spoken.
If I had two wishes, I knew would come true,
I'd give one away and share one with you.

What's the matter? *"Gimme a break,"*
I saw a doctor, he was a fake.

He threaded my needle like he was a weaver,
And charged me a bundle for having Spring Fever!

That's the end of my story, the end of my verse,
My doctor got better; but I got worse.
December 6, 2002 See also Promises and
Pie Crusts, page 250, for a different version!

Saturdays!

Saturdays are best! Bar none.
Enjoying life and having fun.
Hop, skip, dance, run!
Go on and play,
Till it's all done,
Seizing the day!
Chasing the sun!
May 25, 2019

Scheming-Time!

Oh, I could be chasing a moonbeam,
Or tasting _thirty-one_ kinds of ice cream,
Or scheming a new scheme.
But what could be duller!
So, I'll just daydream,
IN LIVING COLOR!
Tuesday, April 14, 2020

September!

If you'd just reflect, my friend,
And recall our love, way back when,
We'd embrace and then,
Say we were wrong,
And sing again,

September's Song!

September! How sweet the sound!
Autumn's colors bursting all around.
I'm heaven bound,
Thanks to my Lord!
Because we found,
Sweet accord!
Long ago,
On June 11, 195-Oh!

Sundays!

Some days tarry, others fade.
This is the day the Lord has made!
My Lord they laid,
On Calvary's tree.
The price he paid,
Set me free.
May 26, 2019

Sunday: The First Day!

Sundays are part of the craze,
In these Coronavirus days,
You'd think crime pays!
But, you dare not run;
The second phase,
Will be less fun.
So,
Mend your ways,
Till it's done!
Sunday, May 24, 2020

Terrible Tuesdays!

I'm glad the bad days are few,
Like Mondays! They're awfully blue.
Thursdays are too!
But,
Not worse by far!
If
You want a clue,
That's a low bar!
Tuesdays are!
April 14, 2020

Thursdays!

Every day is good indeed,
But some days fill a special need,
Just to succeed,
In things that count,
A day to heed,
Thursday's fount.

Time and Tears!

The second Charlie went out to play,
The Piper came and had his say.
But a miracle, it seems, got in the way,
Reluctantly he waits for another day.

And down through the years, when bluebirds sing,
I'll forever remember that bittersweet spring,
When fate had tried to leave a hole,
But God filled it up and touched my soul!
**Charlie's wreck was on April 2, 1991. I wrote this poem on
the first anniversary of that unforgettable tragedy.**

Time and The River!

Nothing's more dependable.
Nor anything more end-able,
Time's bendable!
But
Bad times don't stay.
Time's spendable,
And we pay!

Tuesdays!

Some days just don't seem to fit,
Not much I can do about it.
A little bit,
Out of their place,
Leaving me fit,
For His grace!
May 21, 2019

Wasted Years!

It has been said many times,
Youth is wasted on bad rhymes,
And nickels and dimes.
Early years come,
Ringing life's chimes,
And that's the sum,
Of those wasted times!
May 23, 2019

Wednesdays!

Some folks call it Wednesday's Child,
Full of woe and *"Hump-Day"* beguiled.

I'm not so dialed,
So let it ring,
Stormy or mild,
Or
Most anything!
May 22, 2019

Wednesday! A Freudian Slip!

"Wednesday's Child is meek and mild,"
Someone said of this *mid-week* child.
Now ain't that wild,
A *half-way-blip!*
And thus beguiled.
Sigmund's slip!
May 20, 2020

And finally, I would have never come to the realization that I spend far more time writing about…well, *TIME*, than any other category. Very interesting indeed! Perhaps it's an indication of what I ponder most; but, it could just be that I have way too much *time* on my hands? If not in my mind.

Santa Over Mendocino
**The 1928 Front Page From the Mendocino Beacon where
I was the Newspaper's Court Reporter from 2000-2014.**

CHAPTER 3
Poems for,

HOLIDAYS AND FAMILIES

A Claybrook Christmas!

A
Big
Merry
Christmas
To all of you.
May your holiday
Wishes all come true.
And may you always know,
How very much He loves you,
And always cares for you and yours.
Just pause for a moment and remember
The reason for the season. A baby in a manger,
Who would give His life that you might live forever.
Removing your guilt; but, also removing you from danger.
And, as you leave December to enter the year of our Lord, two
Thousand and Twenty-two, celebrate the New Year with joy unspeakable,
As you bring to Him, the gift that is above every gift…The gift He first gave
You
And
Yours.

His Love and His Life!

Unto us a child is born, Jesus Chris our Lord
Merry Christmas and may you and those you love, have a happy and healthy New Year.

Don Claybrook, Sr. Christmas, Originally in 2017

Life can be so complicated.
We are glad that we can,
Find Full and simple,
But extraordinary
Peace in
Jesus Christ.
We wish you a beautiful
Christmas Season,
Full of Joy that lasts far
Beyond the day that marks
The Savior's birth;
And,
More than ever, we pray
For
Peace on Earth.

Merry Christmas with Love,

Don Claybrook
From my family to yours

• • •

And those you love!

Blueberry Hill!
(And a Christmas Tree for you)

A

Mr.

Domino

Made his

Fortune in

Pizza. Fact is,

You could say he

Made a kill. But sadly,

Our Mr. Domino lost it all,

Where?.....On Blueberry Hill!

Now, what in the world is this sad

Poem talking about? You'll learn the

Answer very soon. Of this happy notion,

I have very little doubt. First, let's consider

The man's first name. Not Mr. Cole. He's one

Of those Nats. In order to understand this poem,

Our man's name is neither Nat nor Pat. It's just Fats.

You're gonna hate me… In fact, you'll likely want to kill.

But I'm just here trying to tell you, No pizza in the world can

Ever

replace,

__Old Blueberry Hill__

December!

Ah, my favorite time of year!
Christmas joy and holiday cheer.
When God draws near,
The Christ-child comes.
Let's make it clear,
Beat the drums!
December 1, 2019

Do Miracles Still happen?

Now Christmas is my favorite holiday by far!
With holiday cheer and Bethlehem's star.
But life is neither not and nor!
Do dreams still come true?
A miracle left the door ajar,
So I believe they do….
Dec. 2, 2019

My Teacher!
(A tribute to Miss Brubaker)

In second grade she said I'd go far,
If I would hitch my wagon to a star.
Well now…that's a pretty high bar!
But her wise words still move me,
Many years after she spoke them.
But it was another star,
You see, Bethlehem's!
That's the star…I reached for!
And
That has made all the difference!
October 28, 2021

Packages (Christmas)

Packages abound at Christmas time,
And I know that joy does too.
Some are red and some are green,
While others are sad and blue.

Tie them with ribbons narrow and wide,
Or bind them to the past.
Tie them so the package won't break,
While in sadness they pray and fast.

Packages abound at Christmas time.
They conceal our real emotions.
They hide the gift in subtle ways,
And conceal the tears of oceans.

He came in a package on Christmas Day,
His wrapping was a manger.
His mother hid him for two long years,
To keep him away from danger.
He was lifted up at Eastertime;
A tomb became his wrapping.
But the gift which the grave concealed,
He offered me with a gentle tapping.

Packages abound at Christmas time,
So many shapes and sizes.
Some are nice like special friends,
But sadly, some are surprises.

It matters not how pretty the ribbon,
When all the trappings are gone.
For pretty is as pretty does.
But ugly goes to the bone.

So give me your gift and I'll give you mine,
As our Christmas' love we renew.
And I'll ponder again, for the millionth time,
When all the wrappings and the ribbons are gone,
What kind of package are you?
<u>Written circa 1987-89, and revised on November 27, 2017</u>

Halloween

Nevaeh Simmons, A Little Bit of Heaven

Indeed, she gets her name from Heaven spelled backwards!
Delightful baby girl and niece of my adopted Reno family,
Dan and Becky Kellett! And a house full of boys!
<u>Photo Credit: Don Claybrook, Sr.</u>

A Kitten Named *"Little Rip"*
A Child's Book for Halloween
A Halloween Tale Inspired by a True Story
Don Claybrook, Sr. Ph.D.
All illustrations in *Little Rip* by Meili Daniel.

Claire was a little girl,
Just seven years old.
She was in second grade,
And did what she was told
(Sometimes!).

She had a little brother,
Donny was his name,
She thought him such a brat.
*"Instead of having a brother,
I'd rather have a cat."*

*"A kitten would be lovely,
A brother a pet is not.
I really want a kitten,
But a brother is what I've got."*

"I wish I had a kitten
Meow! Purr! Run!
But all I have's a brother
And he's no fun."

Suddenly it came to her,
Wow! It was great!
She told Donny about it,
They could hardly wait.

They shouted!
And then they planned their plan.
They plotted!
And now they had it.
And oh, the plan was grand!

And then they talked about it,
The planning of their plan.
"I know Halloween's coming,
And we can 'trick-or-treat,'

And it will surely work out right
Because our plan's so neat."

"Now here is just what we will do,"
Claire told her little brother.
"When Halloween finally comes
I'll share my plan more further."

"I really have a great idea
That I will tell to you.
And no one, but no one,
Will know just what we'll do."

"Claire!" My mom was calling,
She called Donny too.
I wondered what she wanted,
My brother said she knew!
"Oh phoo, she doesn't know!"
My brother was such a brat.
"And if you dare tell her,
We'll never get our cat."

He just shrugged his shoulders,
I doubted that he'd tell,
Cause when he told the last time,
I really rang his bell!

"Oh dear, my lovely children,"
Oh how my mom could fuss.
"You've got to do your homework."
She was always in a rush.

The second time she called us,
Donny really started to run.
He sure wasn't a kitten,
He was no fun!

"Claire, Donny,
Time to eat," said mom
"Time to wash your hands."
She was in the kitchen,
Banging pots and pans.

"Don't you worry," Claire told Donny,
"She knows nothing at all."

And then they heard their dad,
Coming down the hall!
He was really frowning,

As he took off his hat,
And they wondered if he guessed the plan,
The plan about the cat.

"Hello kids! Claire, Donny,
How was your day?" asked dad.
Then bowed his head and thanked the Lord,
For everything they had!

"We don't have everything," Claire thought,
"We don't have a cat."
But then dad said, *"Amen!"*
And that was that, was that!

Claire thought about her kitten,
The one that she was getting.
Oh yes,
The kitten that she was getting.

"Why do the days take so long?
And the nights, they're long too.
When I was just five years old
Oh how the time just flew.

But now that I have a plan
To get myself a cat,
Time doesn't really move at all
But my brother's still a brat!
Oh yes he is!
And I'd rather have a cat."

"September, and then October,"
Their mom announced today.
Claire cried, *"I'm waiting for October*
But September's here to stay!
If October ever comes
Halloween can't be far away.

And when it finally comes,
I'll
Play
Play
Play
I can't wait for that day!"

Finally Halloween came.
Her plan would work for sure.

To get herself a kitten,
All fluffy, white, and pure.

She knew just what she'd name him.
He'd come each time she'd call
And they would romp and frolic,
She'd call her kitten *"Snowball."*

They'd laugh and run and play.
And, that's not all,
They'd really have a ball.

She dressed up like an angel.
Donny was a ghost.
She said, *"Come on let's hurry."*
He stood there like a post.

She said, *"Now what's the matter?*
You know I want a cat."
He said, *"Claire, I don't want to do it."*
"My gosh! What a brat!"
"I don't care," he said
And that was that, was that.

Claire was so mad she couldn't think,
There was nothing she could do.
The plan she'd planned to get her kitten
Would certainly take two.

Her brother, the ghost, looked at her
As he went to *"trick-or-treat."*
Claire stared right back at him,
Wanting their eyes to meet.
But he turned and walked slowly away,
A ghost with little feet.

"Forget my plan, forget my cat
Forget my brother, the little brat.
To make a plan was really dumb.
I really hate him! The little bum."
"Brothers are bad!"
Claire said out loud,
As she joined the Halloween crowd,
An angel heading down the street,
"I might as well "trick-or-treat."

Ring, ring, ring,
She pushed the bell,
And waited for the candy,

"We have nothing to give," They said,
"We have no gum or candy."
Claire thought, *"Now that's just dandy!"*
"No candy?"
No candy!"

"Wait!" they said,
As she stood there in pain,
Looking like she'd been bitten.
Then they came right back
And handed Her
A beautiful baby kitten!

"We have no gum or candy.
Or anything like that.
All we have is this little kitten
Brought home by our cat."

Claire stood there in her angel suit,
Not thinking it was real.
The kitten started licking her.
She stroked him just to feel.

He was so soft and nice and warm,
His fur was smooth and black.
A star streaked across his face,
She couldn't give him back!
So, she put him in her sack.

"But wait!" Screamed Claire,
As she strolled home in the night.
"What am I gonna call him?
'Snowball's' just not right."

And she was quite a sight,
She and her kitten that night.

The kitten started scratching
And making quite a noise,
When suddenly Claire saw Donny
And lots of neighbor boys.

When they saw she had no candy
They laughed and screamed a lot,
But then they saw her sack and
shouted,

"Hey Claire, what you got?"
"Meow!" purred the kitten
And ripped the sack apart.
He stuck his head through the hole
And gave the boys a start.

Donny cried, *"I want him,"*
With a quiver on his lip.
The kitten raised his pretty head
Claire shouted, **"Little Rip!"**

"You want him?" She scolded,
As **"Little Rip"** softly licked her hand,
"Where in the world were you hiding,
When I finally worked my plan?

You wanted to 'trick-or-treat'
To have a lot of fun,
And now you want to share
When all is said and done."

"Claire, I'll split my candy with you."
Begged Donny,
"I'll give you the most."
So, Claire and Donny shared ***"Little Rip,"***
The angel and the ghost.

The End
Written by Don Claybrook Sr. circa 1981-82

After 42 years, I fleshed this poem out, turning it into a 45 page poem, with an additional 15 pages of photos of my family. The longer version was publishing as a Children's Halloween book in September of 2021. Meili Daniels was my illustrator and she did a fabulous job. Please go to Amazon and read the reviews!

And, at the end of another category, we are reminded of how important Holidays are for the family. Indeed, I think they are perhaps the most important days spent in keeping families together. It certainly cannot be Family Reunions! I've found that oftentimes those are just *"One-Up-Manship,"* charades. Or perhaps *"Mal-Functions"* would fit more cogently.

The kids of
A Kitten Called
Little Rip.

Donny and Autumn Claire
Photo by Don Claybrook, Sr. at Lake Tahoe many years after my two kids became adults!

My reflections on concluding this chapter? *Oh, there's no place like home for the holidays*; but, I'm no longer certain as to where home is…or if I ever was.

Liberty Jackson
(Jack) **on her**
21st Birthday, Oct. 25, 2017. Photo credit, Ali Smith, a sorority sister at Chico State.

CHAPTER 4
Poems for,

WOMEN AND GIRLS' BIRTHDAYS

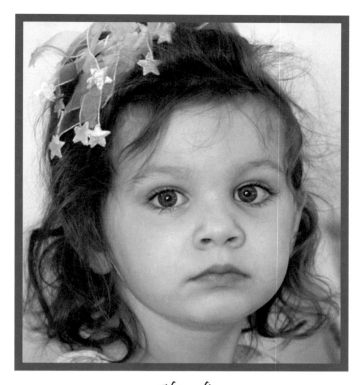

Abigail!
**My only granddaughter, with the most beautiful
Blue eyes I've ever seen!
Abigail Ivie Claybrook on her 3rd Birthday.
Photo by Don Claybrook, Jr.**

Abigail!

While we were at the Louvre, Don Jr's call came.
"We've got a baby girl, Dad! Guess her name."
"Son, is this a game?
Like show-and-tell?"
"Dad, that's so lame!
"It's Abigail!"'
July 30, 2019

Advancing Years!
(Lanora's 82nd)

Dear Sis, you're catching up to me…but don't mope.
You're fine if you can still do the *Rope-a-Dope*.
But at your age, well…that's a very *slippery slope!*
So blow out those 82 candles,
But don't tell the pope,
He might put on his Roman sandals,
And,
Up and elope!
With love, Don

A Girl Named Dorothy Jeanne!

On November *twenty-third*, in 1949, her presence was made known.
Dorothy J. was born…well, because the seed had already been sown!
With very little fanfare she came…the fifth child of Henry and Ruth.
Four siblings had preceded her; but, to add another? How uncouth!

An aunt and a cousin, Dorothy Jeanne was named after a couple of kin,
What was hardly a perfect combination would ultimately become a win.
Her Aunt Dorothy was a rounder…her cousin, Jeanne, a military wife.
D.J. had the names of both given to her, but she hardly had their life.

Her first cradle? A plumbing shop! The other half of it was her home.
But the H. Claybrook's tarried nowhere. Oh, they were born to roam!
T'was in their DNA, an initial identification, back then, unknown well.
Vacations were nice but sinking down roots…now that was pure hell!

We thought that she was anemic…She thought that took a lot of gall!
The months and years passed quickly by, like winter following the fall.
Baby sister was born in Flour Bluff Texas…it was mostly all *"bluff."*
Named for a flour supply ship, its crew was rough, and leather tough.

It capsized and ran aground in Laguna Madre, some say it lost power.
Urban-sprawl and *devil-may-care*, put the *"bluff"* before the *"flour."*
D. J. had become a lovely young lady who had very uncommon sense.
A rare combination, displaying an impressive and a quiet confidence.

Dorothy J., like a couple of her sibs, began to hope, plan and scheme,
Fervently wanting to attend college, thus fulfilling her stardust dream.
She would disdain her spurious anemia, reaching for the distant stars,
Seeking scholarly academia, and bravely fighting, the *"Paper Wars."*

Her first, tentative attempt at marriage, was lost on a dangerous curve,
When she and her brand new husband, tried living their life with verve.
Fate and circumstances joined forces, abruptly conspiring to convene,
Their young romance was shattered, at the bottom of a snowy ravine.

Life and her Lord bowed DJ's head <u>down</u>; but things were looking <u>up.</u>
God was about to send her another. It was divine intervention abrupt!
His name? Mike, sent by another Dorothy, bringing <u>our</u> Dorothy cheer,
Hope that would never disappoint, a love lost, she'd never have to fear.

Our Lord always saves the best for last, if it's life we're thinking about.
He'd do the same for Dorothy and Mike…we never had reason to doubt.
God surely works in wondrous ways, sending Erica, a loving gift of grace.
A *by-product* of His love, and surely a gift they would perfectly embrace.

Erica Noelle was placed in your loving care, *"For such a time as this."*
I recall Queen Esther, and <u>know</u>, God has blessed you with a Holy Kiss!
I thank God upon every remembrance of precious Erica and big Mike,
But remembering my sister on this special day, none other day is like.
It's Thanksgiving!
<u>Written for the occasion of your 68th birthday, November 23, 2017</u>

A Heart of Gold! Rebecca Kellett!

Well, what can I say? Rebecca Kellett turns _forty-five_ today.
She's not going to like it. I expect there'll be the devil to pay.
But, for those of us who've already been to this lonely place,
Only at 60+, can one start begging for God's amazing grace!

Becky, my friend, put on your makeup and wear a sweet grin.
Then just go out and knock 'em dead, that's the only way to win.
Cause one day when you are, say like around about eighty-one,
You'll look in the mirror and cry, _"Lord, what have YOU done?"_

Don't you be surprised if He answers you back, _"Becky, my dear,_
I've been as close as your heart-beat, you've always had my ear.
I've given you three healthy sons, a very good man, and Jordan."
But, if she still says, _Jordain_, then tell her, _"I beg your pardon!"_

Now the serious stuff: I expect there's a bit of silver in your hair.
I know you have a heart of gold. Silver and gold? A lovely pair!
Precious metals, like _worn-out_ robes. You wear them both well.
A good wife is worth more than precious gems, she's not for sell!

So, Rebecca, as you relentlessly press on toward that _Big Five-Oh_!
Please understand how much you are loved by us who really know,
Our Lord never made a better soul than Rebecca (Simmons) Kellett,
You can put that in your pipe and smoke it; or, publish it and sell it.
So today, Rebecca, on number 45, I lift a Coke Zero to you,
(not to indicate your worth),
But simply to say,
"You mean more to me, Becky,
Than most people on God's green earth."
For the occasion of your 45th Birthday, February 7, 2019.

A Sister to Remember!
(Lanora turns 78)

My oldest sister, *twenty-two* months younger than I, turned *seventy-eight* today.
No one knows where all the years went. Some were, perhaps, lost along the way.
Yes, lots of years have come and gone, and many, myriad days have passed,
She's <u>honestly</u> lived her days and nights, some awfully slow, others very fast.

Where do I start, where do I go, to understand this lady, this nearly perfect saint?
I'll do what I can; but, don't expect a masterpiece, like Michelangelo would paint.
She was born on a November day, *twenty-seven* days in….in nineteen *thirty-nine*.
Dad swore that heaven had come down. I thought she was simply a sister of mine.

I heard things like, *"She's as pretty as a picture"* or, *"Just as cute as a bug."*
I'd seen both those. Might as well have said *"Let's sweep her under the rug."*
Now I don't think I was jealous at all, or anything like that. Confused? Maybe.
I'd never been around anyone younger than I, and along comes a new baby!

She was christened *Lanora Ruth Claybrook*, got her middle name from mother.
But, from where in the world, did that first name come? It's a name like no other,
I'm guessing, they just didn't know how to spell *Lenora,* way back in the day,
When all of life was easy, and when not even a single soul, had *the devil to pay.*

The days rolled right on by, leaving dad's favorite, learning to sing her song.
She was growing up just like a flower, blossoming…she could do no wrong.
Becoming a beautiful, delightful young lady, her days were filled with laughter,
Most importantly, she made Jesus Christ her Lord, thus sealing her ever-after.

When Lanora reached high school, Stan had already, rolled away from home,
Les and I, her remaining brothers, and, two sisters, had not yet learned to roam.
That's because I played two years of football, at Mineral Wells High School.
Lanora was my biggest supporter. I believe she thought that I was kind'a cool!

At the games, if I did something good, she would shout, *"Way to go Claybrook!"*
My teammates were confused. This pretty chick was giving me, a very long look.

Cracking up laughing, I quickly told them *"She's nothing to me, <u>just</u> my sister."*
My words must have taken root. From that day on, they just called me, *"Mister."*

When I went off to Baylor, She and those still at home, went to the Golden State.
But, like so many others before them, all the gold was gone, couldn't get a stake.
They picked plums, they picked grapes, knowing Dad, they likely picked a fight.
California was tough, they gave it all they had, and worked with all their might.

But, nothing is harder for a Claybrook, than to say these three words, *"I give up!"*
Lanora yearned for the Land of the Alamo, Texas, to drink again from <u>THAT</u> cup.
Home again! A feeling that has no equal, except for the day that Christ comes in,
When winning or losing lacks meaning, until one is set free, from evil and sin.

She found herself a church home, a refuge in which she could practice her skills,
Harlendale Baptist Church, in San Antonio…she was finally home from the hills.
She met a young man named Richard, a Godsend if there ever was such a thing.
Giving Richard her heart, while he gave her a promise, and a shiny diamond ring.

They then said their vows in marriage, then adopted a baby boy and named him Ric.
He was destined to be successful in every way. Now it was time for the *"hat trick."*
No one could stop the restless flow of years, hastening by with their hopes and fears.
They adopted another baby, they named her Desiree, bringing, a *joyful-kind* of tears.

Lanora and Richard's lives had become a miracle…God blessed from heaven above!
He would finish the *"Hat Trick,"* with *"I'm sending you a song, the Melody of Love."*
Lanora could have no children, soon knew that she was carrying new life, a child,
They named her Karrie, calling Jeremiah 33:3. God's phone number had been dialed!

Call unto Me and I will answer thee, showing you mighty things you know not.
But, Richard and Lanora could not have known then…they had hit the jackpot!
And, as they say, *"The rest is history."* So, Richard, Ric, Desiree, and Karrie,
I thank my God upon every remembrance of you four, but I cannot afford to tarry.
So, my sweet sister Lanora, on this your 78th birthday,
I wish for you the best gift I know!
<u>I wish you love.</u>
<u>For the occasion of your 78th birthday, November 27, 2017,</u>

August 15, 1919!
(Written for my mother)

It was on this inauspicious date, in a year incredibly blessed by our Heavenly Father.
He took an ordinary year and gave it extraordinary meaning! But why did He bother?
Our Lord paused creation, He paid perfect attention, for the making of a perfect pearl.
Why was 1919, not just a mark in time? God wanted to present, a wonderful baby girl!

August was half gone, when she was christened *Willie Ruth*. My gosh! What a name!
Willie Ann and John Thomas were responsible for both…the blame <u>and</u> the shame.
Born in St. Augustine, deep in East Texas, where the evergreen and pine trees sit,
"God put a void in the heart of man," said the Saint, *"where only He will fit."*

So, Ruth grew quickly in wisdom, if rather slowly in stature, becoming a lovely lady,
Life was simple and sweet, each day was so precious, those times were not so weighty.
Her family *make-up* was very normal, for siblings, brothers, Sisters, parents and such,
Ruth's sisters were Beth, Ethel, Bertha, and Theora…..many girls…. but not too much.

Now add three brothers to those six sisters, Ooops! My bad, I just forgot Aunt Nettie.
With so very many mouths to feed, Willie Ann wished that J.T. was J. Paul Getty!
The olden days nine children, *(Ruth's three brothers were Andy, Johnny and Buck),*
Was just about right, they had no birth control; or else, they had some awfully <u>bad</u> luck!

Ruth grew like a sapling always will, and became a child of God through Jesus Christ,
Like millions before her, she' repented; and, with that, her ransom had been priced.
He was reconciling the world to His Father, that whosoever would, might be saved,
She accepted Jesus as her Savior, and it didn't cost a dime, the ransom was waived!

A Christian first, Ruth was also a faithful member, of Oak Street Baptist Church.
Her Sunday School teacher was a brave young man, Henry. He had the perfect perch,
To scope out all of his options, looking for a future mate; But, Ruth was just 15 years old!
Henry Reu was *twenty-two,* seven years older than she, which made him feel oh so bold.

He offered her a diamond ring, with a stone so incredibly small, it could hardly be seen.
Then they were married at Newcastle. Not in England, the one on the road to Abilene.

They began having babies, but like the woman in the shoe, they didn't know what to do.
They ended that project by having Stan, Don, Lanora, Liz, D.J., and Lester Lee too,
Ending all speculation. <u>They knew exactly what to do!</u>

Time traveled just like the wind, neither of which were ever seen, nor would ever cease,
Dad died in '89, Les twelve years later. Our patriarch and favorite son…..Gone in peace!
Peace forged in the crucible of a fiery furnace, it would endure for a long, long time,
Not instantly bringing comfort, fulfillment follows promise, like reason follows rhyme.

Then mom, our precious mother, our origin, quite simply our best friend. God took too,
After many memories and years, the world lost some of its charm, the sky is not so blue.
Back to St. Augustine, the Saint who gave his name, to the town where she was enticed,
To become a child of God and a saint. A member of <u>The Church</u>, the Bride of Jesus Christ.
So, mother, on this the 98th year of your birth, *"Bless'ed"* is what we all call you,
Indeed a saint, as much as anyone who ever lived, your reward is way past due!
Mom, you gave us the greatest gift of all, you taught us the real meaning of LOVE,
Love is patient and kind; and, the Love that never fails, comes from heaven above.
<u>Happy 98th Birthday Mom, on this 15th day of August, 2017</u>
Mom, I long to see you again, and experience, for the first time, a *never-ending* hug,
For that's what mothers do best…..and your six children……were that way blessed.
<u>July 9, 2017…in remembrance of our mother, God's most precious earthly gift.</u>

<u>Becky Turns Two-Score and Seven!</u>

OMG! Are you kidding me? Becky's turning *two-score* and seven!
From where I sit, that's a melody, a tune called *Seventh Heaven!*
I suppose that's better than the normal way to just up and play it.
So, way down deep in my soul, I just have to smile and say it!

I do sadly recall when you turned 37. Why, I was twice your age!
So Becky, just keep on having those birthdays and turn the page.
I'm better off when you have more. Like there's no way I'm 94!
As you grow older I gain, so please have about *five-score* more.

And now, to the serious stuff. Have a great birthday sweet lady!
I always tried to hide from that Hawkin's girl, first name Sadie,

You bless us all, Becky, because you are uniquely one of a kind.
So, I'd never hide from you! No way! I'm not out of my mind!

Carpe Diem, and seize the day and hold on with all you've got.
I'd christen you Dame Rebecca. If I could, a Knight you're not.
You're courageous, you are a wonderful mom, wife and friend.
Your parenting, teaching, faith and love are a beautiful blend,
And,
I'm so happy and so very blessed just to call you, *"Friend."*
Now just between you and me, when God made you,
He threw away the key, into the deep-blue-sea!
January 29 for your birthday on February 7, 2021
Becky was so young, she had to Google Sadie Hawkins!

Birthday in "The Ville!"

Well, Happy Birthday to you! Our beautiful Martha Lee,
You do have a lovely heart which is awfully hard <u>NOT</u> to see!
I wish I were in *"The Ville"* today, to see your smiling face,
Touched by divinity; our Lord's incredible amazing grace!

I think we just might swap you, and, maybe we should.
But then, perhaps we'd refuse to sell you, even if we could!
For only an Arabian Sheik could pay the winning price!
So I'll stick to writing rhymes; stuff like *"Men and Mice!"*

Now if you think <u>this</u> birthday number is hard to take,
Just go on and enjoy your family, ice cream and cake,
Because *for crying out loud,* you ain't seen nothing yet!
Your next number will seem about like the National Debt!

But I won't mention the years; you know which one it is!
So, turn on that sweet smile that says, *"It's nobody's biz!"*
When your friends ask you, *"Martha, which one is this?"*
Just stand back and laugh as they cry, moan and hiss.

May your day, Martha Lee, be as wonderful as you are,
As you hitch your life's wagon to some near or distant star,
And may my love for you, take refuge in your sweet heart,
For our friendship will always be, the most incredible part!
God did it all….from the start!
When an O.U. chuckwagon fell apart!
Happy Birthday, Sweet Lady
Martha Lee died a tragic death near Waco Texas on April 10, 2021.

D.J. On Turning 69!

Dorothy Jeanne's birthday, what fun!
On Thanksgiving Day, just add one.
Evokes my pun!
Crying out loud!
The hard years done.
She stands proud.
11/20/2018 for your birthday, November 23, 2018

Dorothy Jeanne at Sixty-Nine!

She was born on an autumn day around Thanksgiving time,
Dad said he wouldn't trade her for a single *Yankee Dime*.
Dorothy Jeanne was the fifth child out of six Claybrook kids.
That was a whole lot of don'ts, but also quite a few dids.

Historically, she was born on the eve of the Korean War.
By then, we were almost rich. Even had a new, used car!
She had two older sisters who brought her sundry joys,
But her clear favorites were the three Claybrook boys.

Her dad was named Henry, some just called him H.R.
He was a prophet, a plumber, and a *rounder* in a bar.
Just reverse the order and you can see his life's curve,
A smattering of vigor and vim and a whole lot of verve.

Her mother was Ruth, a lady with the patience of Job,
Who lived all her life with class, like a *well-worn* robe.
She never had very many of those…just one at a time,
But to her six children, she looked far beyond sublime.
Stan, their firstborn….was healthy, hearty and strong.
Don was their last…well, until four more came along.
Dad, always looking over his shoulder for a new moon,
Don was fifth from last. That's the name of that tune.

Now Lanora came about 22 months after number two.
She was the apple of Dad's eye, and he did have a few.
That *"Moon watching"* had paid off once again it seems.
It was over his shoulder, but never far from his dreams.

Elizabeth was fourth in this lineup of the 10 *most-wanted,*
Just five years before our Birthday Girl came undaunted.
Both were born on the *twenty-third* day of November,
A day which time and tide cannot help but remember.

The last of the Claybrook kids was a boy named Lester Lee.
We all loved him and clung to him as bark does to a tree.
We all questioned God's timing, Les was gone all too fast.
But someone so sweet and innocent never seems to last.

And now your special day is far-spent my dear baby Sis.
I love you now like I did then. It's never been hit or miss.
I hope you realize, like I did after so much toil and strife,
The last of the journey is a gift, much like the first of life.
So chase it, face it and embrace it. You've earned it.
Happy Birthday! DJ
Written on November 20, 2018 on the occasion of your 69th birthday, November 23, 2018

DJ Turns 70!

My baby sister, DJ,
Is turning 70 in Playa del Rey!
And so I say,
To lift you up,
Drink up today,
Drain your cup!
__November. 23, 2019__

Lanora Ruth!

Well now, another year is gone, but where did it go?
Seems like it's more fleeting than a dusting of snow.
Knowing the provenance of space and passing of time,
As futile as recapturing the sound of love's sweet chime.

Oh, poets and philosophers have tried to understand it.
It's kind of like trying to know how the stars were lit.
Go on, give it a guess, give it a try, but time has a stitch.
Might as well try scratching seven years' worth of itch!

But, a year in your life did pass, inexorably going south;
So, you just might as well be up…as down in the mouth.
Cause Tuesday, November 27th, you'll be _seventy-nine,_
And none of you <u>older</u> siblings want to hear you whine!

Now, I'm not being cruel or mean…I couldn't if I tried,
22 months ago I was the age you are today…and I cried.
I tried my best to stop it. Time wasn't serving me so well,
But that trip isn't paved, as the way is from here to hell.

With much fear and trembling, here's my recommendation.
Accept it as my gift to you, with neither fear nor trepidation,
Grab a friend and go out and have a big filet mignon steak,
With lots of good sides of everything that restaurants make.

But let nothing cross your mind, like calories or some such,
As Henry Claybrook would say, *"That'll get you in Dutch!"*
Add dessert to top it off; but, about the price don't even dicker,
For I can assure you, your 81st, will get here much quicker!
Happy Birthday Lanora,
Written on November 22 for the occasion of your 79th birthday on November 27, 2018

Maria!

Man-o-live,
75!
It's a day just to,
Shuck and jive.
Raise your hand,
And I'll give you five.
Cause we two,
Just Staying Alive!
Composed Sept. 13, 2017 for your birthday,

Mother at 70!

At mixing metaphors, I do delight,
Like *He's so blind! He's out of sight*
I cleaned his bell, He rang my plow,"
"A purple moon jumped a harvest cow."
T
Three score and ten; now that's not bad.
That's twenty more than I've ever had.
So, with some *Sunsweet*, and a bit of luck,
You'll do more, than just *pass* the buck.

You know how to make a wet hen sore?
Double *thirty-three*, and then add four.
That wasn't so tough, new math aside.
Age waits for neither time nor tide.

When one turns seventy, what-a-ya do?
You don't give her candy…too tough to chew.
You don't give *the gift that keeps on giving.*
Pushing up daisies is not for the living.

There was a young lady who lived in a stew.
Had 6 children; knew not what to do…evidently.
Something most suave from your very own six.
Arriving any day now, like *a much-needed fix.*
U.P.S. or Federal Express,
They might bring a ring; or, perhaps a dress.
But if the weather is cold and bitter,
You can think the hunter who killed this critter.

You'll stay really warm, like wool on a sheep,
And *shake your tail like Little Bo Peep.*
You can wear it at work, you can wear it at play.
You can wear it to go; or, wear it to stay.

But if you're in line for government cheese,
Leave it at home…. it's better to freeze.
It might be wool; it might be tweed.
If you look real close, you'll find a lead.

Ladies who wear them, are pretty in pink.
If I say any more, I'm a genuine fink.
It comes from us six; but just like the rabbits,
We've all fallen prey, to domestic habits.

So, multiply by two…a dozen to say,
Many happy returns, on your special day.
August 15, 1989

OMG! Becky K is 48!

Today Becky K begins her 49th year!
Can a woman that age still get a date?
You're kidding me! Get out of here!
Well, I guess we'll just have to wait.
With Karma looking more like fate?
Every year!
What I'm saying is, I turned 36 more,
Just seven days ago on February first!
And now I've quit even keeping score,
Because that bubble is about to burst!
Things are going from best to worst!
However;
Becky is two days younger every day,
In all those ways that really do count.
She will never have the devil to pay,
As the days, months and years mount,
Because she sips from the Lord's fount!
So Becky,
Seize this day, it's *caper diem* true:
Nobody has the grounds or desire,
To pick a fight or quarrel with YOU!
So long as you keep that special fire,
That's as faithful as heaven's choir!
Our Lord will bring you through!
And you…will be singing too!
Happy Birthday, Sweet Lady!
Becky Kellett's *48th* Birthday, Feb. 7, 2022

One of God's Favorites

When God tweaked His creation plan,
He went the extra mile with JoAn.
"Maybe" is *"Can"*
With this Dear friend.

No *"Also-Ran,"*
A *God-send!*
On the Occasion of JoAn Blackstone's birthday
September 16, 2021

Remembering Your Forty-Sixth!

When does time start again…after it's been put on hold?
When everything's been said, but very little's been told.
How do you think it all went wrong? I cannot explain.
I've looked for answers; but, my search has been in vain.

Of a special birthday, your *forty-sixth,* I remember well,
You were still picking up sticks. Does that ring a bell?
You and Jim at Frank Fat's, invited my lovely lady and I,
To indulge in honey gold prawns, for which I still would die.

We lived life to the limit, we had everything one could want,
I cannot remember it all. Some things I do, and others I don't.
But, as surely as Capistrano beckons; the swallows never delay.
They simply return. And time, like the river, slips right on away!

Now as we enter our *"Golden Years,"* I find myself obsessing,
Years a prelude to death…a time for repenting and confessing.
If the saying is true, that time can be captured in a bottle,
I'll drink deeply from that flask, living my life *full-throttle.*

So now, you and I find our lives in a strange, unfamiliar place,
Where there seems to be nothing, neither love nor amazing grace.
Brothers and sisters are meant to have a very special kind of love,
Where DNA means…not so much…but a relationship from above.

So my dear sister, today, when the calendar marks your 73rd year,
I thank God for <u>what we had</u>. The memories, I celebrate with a tear.
Please, on <u>this</u> 23rd day of the penultimate month…remove the veil.
And see how much I love you…a love from above that will <u>never</u> fail.

Recalling fondly, the joy that we once shared!
Written on this 3rd day of August, 2017, for you my sister, for the occasion of your 73rd
birthday, November 23, 2017. As my poem comes to an end, my prayer and fervent desire is
that our friendship will last for eternity; and, unlike my poem, will never come to an end

Still Picking Up Sticks
(On the occasion of Lib's 46th)

Forty-six and still picking up sticks,
And scheming your little girl schemes,
Like slumber parties out of time,
And gala affairs all sublime,
And dreaming your little girl dreams.

How could you be *forty-six,* little sister of mine?
When I'm six years older than you, and I'm just *thirty-nine!*
Could it be we've forgotten some days that left their mark in time?
Or could it be that you are *forty-six*, and I'm seven years behind?

You came after Stan, me and Lanora, and before D.J. and Les.
You were the first of the last three and followed by two the best.
Austin was first, your bed was the topic, indeed you slept in a drawer,
A training ground *second-to-none*, for learning to sleep in a car.

Colorado was fun a few years later, the highlight was a tire that went flat.
But t'was a vacation all the same, *"You can thank your brothers for that!"*
Flour Bluff was good for a few laughs; you heard what you chose to hear.
For once on a field trip…God forbid, your teacher was having a beer!

In Perin? Well, the price was right, as we searched so hard for a tree.
Christmas would be a silent night, unless we could get one for free.
But hard times bring good memories, when you're broke and out of luck,
We found the best of all those trees, more limbs than an *8-point* buck!

California was waiting, your life to shape, as you came without a clue.
Pacific and the *"Miracle Mile,"* and do you remember our *Miss Blue*?

High school at Franklin was gone, quicker than a duck can go *"quack."*
Off you went chasing your dreams with a Pinto strapped to your back.

You met a man who was in TV, or at least, he sold an antenna or two,
Could spin a yarn or pull your leg, spinning and pulling appealed to you.
You became his wife and adopted a baby girl, Jennifer filled every day.
You had everything; so, what can I say? Then our Lord sent you J. Clay.

And now your life is near perfect, your skies, all incredibly blue.
Forty-six and still picking up sticks, and in your prime it seems.
And I'm thanking my God upon every remembrance of you,
As you dream your little girl dreams.
Happy 46th Lib!
Nov. 23, 1990.

Sweet Jordan Brown!

Well, my sweet Jordan, you have finally hit that magical year,
One you'll celebrate with a few friends, and a whole lot of cheer.
You were born on the seventh day of September, in the year 1996,
Only a few short years ago, still playing the game, *Pick-up Stix*.

Twenty-one! So now you're a woman, and legal on matters weighty.
I've known you only a few years; but, you've <u>always</u> been a lady.
The years gone by, count for a lot, but making your life one big swirl.
Jordan, you'll do wonderful things; so, I simply say, *"You go girl."*

God, gave you three wonderful brothers, the J-Man, Cael and Double K.,
A wonderful mom and step-father…Could you ask for more? No way!
God's Holy Word says you were wonderfully made, on that we all agree.
I thank my Lord on every remembrance of you, as I bow on bended knee.

So Jordan, our Love, what more could you want as I ponder what to give,
You've been blessed with so much talent, you have all your life yet to live.
I don't have much money; so I'll give you a small piece of heaven above.
I'll give you, on your special day Jordan, the greatest gift I've ever known,

I give you the gift of love.
August 7, 2017
For the occasion of your 21ˢᵗ birthday. September 7, 2017

The Big 8-Oh!

My Sis Lanora, third in line,
Just marking years and doing fine,
Had her ducks in line,
Was going strong.
But along came time,
And did her wrong!
November. 27, 2019

The Years Mount

For GG on her birthday 71ˢᵗ birthday! And D.J. on her 73ʳᵈ
As we grow older, the years mount,
The bubbles aren't as effusive from life's fount.
What to do?
Well, for starters,
Just don't count!
That'll get you in Dutch!
Simply dismount,
(With a little help from your crutch!)
It won't hurt!
Much.
Written on a palindrome 12/2/21

At the end of this section, I'm reminded of…well…I just stopped to get a drink of O.J. and I forgot what I'm reminded of…Oh yeah! It reminds me of how little time, since COVID entered our lives, I get to be with my kids, grandkids, sibs and best friends! But if I had to choose how I would die between COVID and Shingles, I'd likely choose the former. But that's probably only because I've had latter. Don't laugh. Have you ever had an itch you can't scratch? I'm pretty sure that's what Native Americans used on the tips of their arrows!

Caelan, Dan, Jase and Kieran

My Kellett Boys, with Dad, Dan Kellett! The kid to the left is scheming something; Dan is wondering if mace is legal to use on boys; the next one is Jase…which actually rhymes with mace; and, to my right is Super K! Eat your hearts out ladies!

Photo credit, Becky Kellett (My *ex-friend! And the boys' Mom, and Dan's better half).* I don't know what I could have said!

CHAPTER 5:
Poems for,

MEN AND BOYS' BIRTHDAYS

A Boy Named Jase!
(5ᵗʰ Birthday)

He's turning five years old today, this boy,
And he's doing it with a smile on his face.
To be sure, he's his daddy's pride and joy,
And his darling mother's sweet embrace.

This young child has a brother named Cael,
And a sister named Jordan, or is it Jordain?
But either spelling will work out quite well,
Each goes together like wet does with rain.

Oh, but then there is that other young lad,
In my opinion, he's just plain old *Double-K*.
That's Kieran Kellett, the first boy they had,
And each is unique in his own special way.

Now, you're God's gift from heaven above,
He created you, and they named you Jase.
You bring such joy, life and incredible love,
All the result of our Lord's Amazing Grace!
April 16, 2018 for the occasion of your 5ᵗʰ birthday, April 29, 2019

Cael Turns 14!

Cael J, you turn 14 today!
What more is left for me to say?
(Words get in the way.)
How then to convey, *"I love you?"*
It's either say or pay.
But I haven't a clue?
I'll just go with the tried and true,
On this, your special day.
Happy Birthday to You!
June 22, 2021

<u>Caelan James Kellett</u>
(<u>June 22, 2007</u>)

Hey C.J., What can I say? It's your big day today.
And, what's more, if I have anything about it to say.
Turning eleven is no small feat. It's a really big deal!
So, let's all just celebrate bigtime, but keep it real.

I suppose I could call you Xi, or maybe Fi or Guy!
But quite honestly, that's not at all the way I fly.
Because then I'd be getting into Chinese checkers,
I prefer *bi-planes.* You know, those *double-deckers.*

So with another jamming year under your old belt,
Just keep on playing with the tiles you were dealt,
While studying letters…….and dictionary looking,
You'd better be studying Scrabble! Not Cooking!

May all your vowels be E's and you consonants X's,
Reminds me of Shirley, my former wife in Texas,
And if God should grant you <u>that</u> *seven-letter* word,
Just thank Him for making you a what? Dirty bird?
Happy Birthday Cael
We all rejoice in you today!
<u>June 22, 2018</u>

<u>Dan the Man!</u>
(40<u>th</u> Birthday)

So, Dan, today is your birthday; and, it is a very special year,
At last hitting the *Big Four-O*, let me make something clear.
If you think the first 40 were fast, you ain't seen nothing yet!
Forty more will fly right on by, like riding a supersonic jet!

But, stop! Let's not go there, let's take a moment and reflect.
Looking back on yesterday can be healthy; let's not neglect.

At God's time, and in His place, you met your beautiful wife!
Our Lord kept His promises, giving you Becky and eternal life.

Three boys, all of them super heroes, Caelan, Kieran, and Jase!
When all get their groove on, a person ponders! Perhaps mace?
These 3 would circumvent it, and you'd love them even more,
I promise, never a dull moment. And you, they'd never bore.

And of course, remember your lovely step-daughter Jordan,
So much like her mother, two pretty flowers, in a rose garden.
Just keep on reflecting on fond memories of yesterday's wine,
Apply the lesson to tomorrow. It will save you a stitch in time.

Dan, you sought and found God's incredible amazing grace,
Yet, you wondered, how Jesus Christ could take your place.
Rev. Dick Coolidge said, *"Son, just tell Him you're a sinner,
That you're sorry for your sins; then, invite Him for dinner."*

Dick surely had Revelation, chapter three, verse twenty in mind,
When he gently told you Dan, to invite Christ to come and dine.
Keeping His promise, when He said, *"I'll sup this cup with you,
I will come again…because, your reward, will have come due."*

"The greatest story ever told," He wants to become your friend.
Dan, you opened up your heart, and humbly invited Christ in.
Then, a miracle occurred; and, I knew it wasn't just some show,
For I was there when it happened, and I guess I ought to know.

Dan Kellett, my friend, just keep on keeping on, what you do best,
When hard times come, talk to your Lord, and let Him do the rest.
As you embark on your *forty-first* year, my prayers are with you.
And I'll be praying that this coming year, God will surely bless,
When all your problems will be but a few
And all of your dreams will surely come true.
Now that's happiness!
Written August 9, 2017,given on your 40th birthday,

Dan Turns 44!

Dan Kellett is having a birthday…AGAIN!
Some are destined to lose and some to win.
But Dan is not one of those losers,
Why? Because *Dan the Man,*
Is one of those choosers.
Find a better dad if you can,
Or a better friend to his fellowman.
You're wasting your time on a trivial pursuit,
Like a hunter who hasn't a clue how to shoot!
But the best thing Dan ever did,
Was not choosing to be a *first-class* techie.
Nope! It's when he made the winning bid,
On a beautiful lady named Becky!
So Dan, go and celebrate your 44 years,
And raise a glass of Champaign, or a couple of beers.
And lift one, if you will, for me,
And thank the Lord that you're not 83!
And for 39 more years…you won't be!
Happy Birthday, my friend,
May your back be always,
With the wind!
On the occasion of your birthday, written Aug. 17, 2021, modified 8/30/21

Factor in the Fudge!

Hey Brandt, share with the group!
No one should be out of the loop,
Just because you refuse to budge
To share,
This platter of chocolate fudge.

But,
It's gonna taste so very good,
Don't agree? Well I wish you would.
But, I guess that's for you to judge.
If I must, I'll give you a nudge.
For,
For I'm too old to hold a grudge.
Nevertheless,
Happy Birthday Brandt…And we all say,
God Bless You on this your special day.
On year 70-Something or another!
Have a good one,
My Brother!
March 14, 2018

Five Years Beyond!
(Caelan James Kellett's 12th Birthday)

By now it's abundantly clear, I only pay a dollar per year.
Have no fear. Just don't want you buying a *6-pack* of beer!
So with that money in mind, just leave the amount behind,
Don't go into it blind, just dwell on the good ties that bind.

Today is your birthday Caelan, and you're turning twelve,
Just *five years beyond* seventh heaven, still on the shelve.
The only thing that would make this day a bit more nifty,
(Given what I pay) is that you wish you were turning $50,
*
Cael, you are one amongst a precious few who have found,
A very special place in my life and in my heart.
Happy Birthday!
12
And if you should ever hit the century mark, go look for your money at a Financial Park!
Written for Caelan on May 21, 2019,
On the occasion of your 12th birthday, June 22, 2019

Jase Turns Six!

The date's in place for young Jase,
April *twenty-nine's*, smiling face!
Keep up the pace,
Stand up and cheer!
Running the race,
Six this year!
Written April 11, 2019, marking the date of your birth, April 29, 2013
Happy Birthday, Little Buddy!

Jase Turns 8!

There was a cool young man named Jase,
A third son, but was born in fourth place.
Who lived on William's Avenue in Reno,
Where the Kellett's *"play"* more than Keno.

Jase Thomas, in the year of our Lord, 2013.
He's one of the nicest kids I've ever seen!
So do your math! This year he turns eight!
Now, he's gonna think he can stay up late!

Well Jase, I got some bad news for you, Son!
You'll want to sleep till all the dark is done!
When you've lived many, many more years,
You'll be reading the clock with your ears!

Enjoy your special day, like no one's seen.
Before I can say *"Presto!"* You'll be a teen,
Remember, I held you when you were one!
Now I'm headed toward the *setting sun*!

Happy eighth Birthday, young man!
Fourth child of parents Becky and Dan!

The *Kellett-Four* were given the best.
Now our Lord will take care of the rest!
April 20·2021,

Kieran Mischa Kellett!

(15)

He was born in the merry, merry month of May,
And I'm fond of calling him just old *Double-K*.
He's turning fifteen today. Bank on it and sell it!
In 2003, was christened Kieran Mischa Kellett.
15! You gotta be kidding! His parents are sighing.
I'm telling the truth! Perhaps you think I'm lying?
Then check the DOB on his birth certificate friend,
And it's 10 to one that I'm sure to win…again.

Kieran hits a *ping-pong* ball like a Texan tells lies,
Or like McDonald's slaps you with all them fries.
Fore you know what's hit you, you're down *15-love,*
Begging Kieran for mercy, as push turns to shove.

So *Double-K*, enjoy your special day, May 8,
And know that we celebrate on this special date.
Because, you see, when we say you're *15-love,*
We mean you're 15 today and blessed from above.
On the occasion of your 15ᵗʰ birthday, May 8, 2018

Kieran Turns 18!

Kieran, has it really been eighteen years already?
I suppose at this age you're feeling rather heady!
Do you feel the burdens of being Number One?
Then you should try being the number two son!
That's no fun!
I know something about that, and so does Cael.

He might just tell you to go jump in a dry well,
I could've used another word, but I'll just cease.
Don't want to get harassed by the *Parent-Police.*
Best make peace!
Let's see, you're starting your nineteenth year.
A concept your mother can't make stand clear!
You'll think you're all footloose and fancy free,
Chasing the young ladies up a sweetheart tree.
Believe you me!
But, there's a sad caveat that I must lay down,
Becoming a man is like a verb without a noun!
All action and no substance is what I'm saying.
You'll have mom and dad kneeling and praying,
A foundation laying!
But, Kieran, you've never disappointed us before,
So here's a tip before you walk through that door.
There are temptations you'll need to renounce.
Like making lots of money in hills and mounts,
But,
Making a difference…is what ultimately counts!
May our Lord go with you.
On the occasion of your 18ᵗʰ birthday, May 8, 2021

Kieran Turns 83 minus 65!
(It's not Rocket Science!)

When a young man reaches eighteen,
It's OK to celebrate and vent his spleen!
Eighteen only comes once in every life.
Might as well get rid of all that strife,
Before he takes a wife,
That is!
I remember well when I turned eighteen.
Before I wore Baylor's gold and green!
In fact, I was a senior at Mineral Wells High,

And my hopes went all the way to the sky.
In the Sweet Bye and Bye!
So Kieran, remember you are very unique,
I'm not talking about your manly physique!
<u>Your</u> difference can be found in <u>your</u> heart,
That's where eternity will always start.
It sets <u>you</u> apart.
I want you to know how special you are!
Our Lord set you aside to make you a star.
To do anything in life, that you want to do,
Only He can make good dreams come true.
And turn pewter skies to blue.
So, Kieran, on this, your very special day,
My hopes for you are real, come what may.
I pray that our Lord will *sunlight* your path.
In 66 years you'll turn every <u>*want*</u> into <u>*hath!*</u>
But don't you dare....check my math!

<u>**On the occasion of your 18th birthday, May 8, 2021**</u>

<u>Lester Lee Claybrook!</u>

He was born on May twenty-ninth, 1953, in Corpus Christi by the Sea,
The day Sir Edmund Hillary scaled Mt. Everest, the very first to do so.
I named him for a preacher, Brother Roloff, first two names Lester Lee,
We soon knew Lester Lee was smart as a whip. How far would he go?

He grew up strong in body and in mind, loving to learn and loving life!
Vicki would become his once and forever love and his wonderful wife.
They had two children, Jason and Andrea....a beautiful pair to be sure,
Learning to love the Lord and how to live a life that was good and pure.

Both of them created quite a stir, the Preacher and this Claybrook boy,
Preaching the Truth and wrestling in Green River, bringing lots of joy!
Years passed by, Jason and Andrea were turning into woman and man,
Les became a plumber, a soldier, computer whiz! Never an *also-ran*.

Fate would then strike an incredibly hurtful and ultimately fatal blow.
And all his family had to go where no family ought ever have to go.
Lester Lee was taken from us way too soon at the age *forty-seven*,
But we'll meet him by and by when we all gather together in heaven.

Les, you were a very good man, a wonderful father, brother and son.
The world is a much darker place now that you've had your final run.
But when I think of the good times we had, it's never the bad I recall,
It's the good days we had in winter, and spring, and summer, and fall!

You were, and are, a brother of whom I can always be so very proud,
Now as I come to the end of this tribute, I confess, I'm crying out loud.
On this the day you would have been *sixty-six*, we miss you so much.
Not long ahead in God's own future, we will definitely get in touch!
I love you Les…and Stan.
You two are the brother that every man should have.
Lester Lee and Stan the Man!
For Les, my youngest brother!

My Buddy, Cael, Turns 10!
(On his 13th Birthday)

Happy 10th birthday, Buddy!
No time to be *fuddy-duddy*.
Now that's bloody,
Cael turning ten.
Something's muddy,
Once again.
So, take this $10 and have some fun,
But stay out of downtown Reno
Without your gun!
(Disclaimer: That's a pun.)

On Turning Eleven!
(Caelan James Kellett)

He was born on June 22, 2007, James Kellett, first name Cael,
This beautiful day in early summer was turning out quite well.
And now his birthday is coming up real soon. He'll be eleven.
We've all learned in real time, when God sent this child Caelan,
He sent a little bit of heaven.
The early years passed quickly, gone forever, lived but just once,
Looking back with sweet memories, the days turned to months,
And as the months turned to years, we thought, *fee, fie foe fum*.
But suddenly we were awakened by the beat of another drum.
And so,
Another brother arrived somewhere in time, *Jase* was his name.
Now there were three boys. None of them were at all the same.
Cael was no longer the baby! All kids not last go thru this phase.
He would slowly grow; but for a while he went around in a daze,
Lost in a maze!
Oh, I could talk about some of Cael's other pursuits, like Scrabble.
That day when he challenged me, it was more like *psycho-babble*.
There seemed to be no *time-limit* in this altogether verbose game,
If one loses, he only has his little remaining bit honesty to blame.

Now Cael's attention would turn to less trivial pursuits. Soccer!
It turned out to be a good fit, much like a Spaniel fits a Cocker.
What I'm trying to say is, C.J. seemed to have wind in his sail,
Making other players look about as slow as a handicapped snail.

That more or less brings us up to date with this guy named Cael.
Wishing him a Happy Birthday while hoping we've hit the nail.
And offering a piece of advice born out of the wisdom of living.
Cael, we love you so much; and, with humility we say,
Happiness comes only in the simple act of giving.
May 26, 2018 on the occasion of your 11th birthday.

"Stan the Man!"

Fortunate is the man who has a big brother,
A little brother too. Yes, I am graced like no other,
Stanley and Les! My brothers are friends of mine.
Just to be in the middle, is a blessing quite divine.

Stanley's appearance came….when Hitler was on the rise.
Yes, they knew Stanley was coming. It was no big surprise.
A cool October evening, nineteen hundred and *thirty-five,*
Mom and Dad together, simply trying to keep hope alive.

Now, my big brother was christened *Stanley Rue Claybrook*,
Dad's middle *"Reu,"* although differently spelled, he took!
He was named for Stanley Peavey, Dad's favorite banker,
For mischief and excitement, Stanley really had a hanker.

Stanley had a rough patch of luck, somewhere about that time,
The odds for his survival, were not worth a Continental dime.
His pneumonia was so very bad, they chose to call it *"double."*
But God was good, and in His love, stayed Stanley's trouble.

His demons came in other ways, a bully called him *Pee-Wee.*
Dad's advice? *"Pick your fights wisely, that should be the key.*
Just keep your head held up proudly, and take it like a man."
Then, for the very first time, Stanley became simply *"Stan."*

I've shared with you Stan's day and year of birth, way back when,
But miracles will never cease, Stan was seeking…to be *born-again.*
Stan told Dad that he was frightened, that he wanted to be saved.
Dad said, Christ was <u>The Way</u>, the road had already been paved.

Stan cried and he pleaded, as he begged for God's amazing grace,
While never understanding, why Jesus Christ would take <u>his</u> place.
Dad said, *"Son, you don't have to beg. Just tell Him you're a sinner,*
That you're sorry for your sins, and invite Him to come to dinner."

Dad must have had Revelation, chapter three, verse twenty in mind,
When he told him to invite Jesus Christ to come, and with Him dine,
Our Lord kept His promise when He said, *"I'll sup this cup with you,
And when I come again, I will give you, the reward that you're due."*

"He's the greatest story ever told. He wants to become your friend."
My brother Stan opened up his heart, and humbly invited Christ in.
How do I know a miracle occurred, that it wasn't just some show?"
Because I was there when it happened, and I guess I ought to know.

Stan was quite a runner, a quarter miler; and, a prequel to Usain Bolt.
When his challengers were way out front, they were in for quite a jolt.
About *one-hundred* and ten yards to go, Stan would really turn it on,
And he'd pass all the competition ahead, like they were made of stone.

Down on the Gulf of Mexico, in Corpus Christi, Stan met his wife to be,
He knew with all his being and all his heart, Margaret Ann held the key,
To all that he held dear, his heart, his soul, his Lord, and family, his life,
That Margaret Ann Houser needed to be, his *"always and forever"* wife

Stan's other brother was Donald *(that's me),* they just called him Don,
Stan became a plumber, but big, little brother, wandered hither and yon.
Don was Stan's middle brother…originator of this biographical verse.
Stan returned to God's Country; but, Don just went from bad to worse.

But first they both went west to find their fortune, to California they came,
Tasting modest success, and failure, they flickered out, as a dying flame.
Stan went back home to the land he loved dearly, land of his father's Texas.
And so, with his partner, Margaret Ann, back to the land of all Don's exes.

Stan, on this your 81st birthday, you've been more than my older brother.
You've been a friend, a husband and a father, an inspiration like no other.
On this special day, I wish for you my brother, my hero in so many ways,
<u>*I WISH YOU LOVE*</u>. It will sustain and carry you, all your *"forever days."*
<u>Epilogue</u>
So, my dear brother, you're no longer Stanley, or *Pee-Wee,* or even plain old Stan.
<u>Today, on July 16, 2017, I christen you, *"Stan the Man"*</u>

You Win…Again! Cael!

Well now, it's Don again, Cael,
Dr. C. back to pay your bail.
With you in jail,
You'll need $3 more.
I'll bite the nail!
And send four.
Yes! I knew it was your 13th, you see,
So my conscience got the best of me.
I was trying to get by with a ten!
Then, I repented of my sin.
And passed the bucks again!
On the occasion of
Your monumental 13th birthday, June 22, 2020

By the time I arrived at the end of this chapter, I was glad that God made little boys and men. But I'm absolutely ecstatic and raptured over the fact that God also made little girls and ladies! I suppose one could say that I'm not quite *gender neutral*, not yet! What a difference a gender makes! Never mind a day! Want me to count the ways? It'll take days…

CHAPTER 6
Poems about,

CELEBRATIONS, RECOGNITIONS, TRIBUTES

A Poem For D.J.!
My Baby Sister

Well, what can I say, DJ?
I hope you're having a good day!
But, come what may,
'Tis oh so true,
I wish to say,
I love you!
May 14, 2019

Brighter Hues!
(Lanora and Deej)

Yesterday was a day like few others have been,
With its every breath just a *'singing the blues.*
But yesterday stayed but *24-four* hours and then,
My mind fled inexorably back to brighter hues.

I don't think I will ever know what it was about,
A day with its fears, heartaches and sad grunge,
A mind working up a bushel of buzz and doubt,
My heart soaking it up like a *brand-new* sponge.

But now He's given me <u>*this*</u> day, the one He made,
Oh, to be sure, He made yesterday too, I confess.
And so, I thank Him that yesterday hadn't stayed,
Now that I've time to reflect, ponder and assess.

I thank my Lord upon every remembrance of a few,
And can honestly say, as I put this sad tale to rest,
Yes indeed, I also thank Him for sisters like you two,
Causing me to recall that I am extremely blessed,
With two of our Lord's very best.
September 13, 2018

Bud and Don Revisited!

Don and Bud's forever friendship, goes way back in time.
Bud's days were filled with fun, and a whole lot of sublime.
Each has sundry and fond memories; and all of them apply.
Don's past was often OK: but, the sad facts, he won't deny.

Bud's dad brought his wife and kids, when stationed at NAS.
Don's dad? A preacher and plumber. Oh my Lord, what a mess!
Drifting happily along, wherever the storm winds would blow,
The boys were in seventh grade; and, had their wild oats to sew.

The two played junior high football down in the old Southwest.
Farrar found a rare Penny; but, I digress, and will later invest.
Bud was center to Don's quarterback, in the big state of Texas.
Don just pondered his fate in life; and, dreamed of all his exes.

Years buzzed by; and, Bud and Don lost touch with each another.
Don played ball for Mineral Wells High; and, looked no further.
Bud went out west where he found his talents were for *round-ball;*
He was given the key to his city…Don was answering The Call.

The rivers just rolled into history; and, Farrar and Claybrook did too.
They married, had kids. Bud sired how many? I'm betting quite a few.
Many years and three wives later, Don fathered three girls and a boy,
Being a father comes with its own blessings. Children were their joy!

Forty-seven years passed; and, these two guys could now look back.
Don went west and remarried, and he went *From a King to a Jack*.
The other went from the army, to a cop and to instructor of teachers.
They made their mark and left it, because both were *over-reachers*.

Together again, Don's knows the truth, now that the story's been told.
He'd found it in his coin book. *That* Penny was worth more than gold!
Bud learned that his future wife he'd stumbled upon, was rare indeed.
And as faithful as a wife can be. I'm jealous, and that I rightly concede.

Now my reminiscing comes to an end; and, I'm as sure as sure can be,
The swallows always return to Capistrano, like leaves do to the tree.
Old friends are like old pennies, they come full circle when they roam,
Having friends like Bud and Penny...as precious as hearth and home.
December 14, 2017 in Fort Bragg, California

Bud's Real Birth Date!

It turns out it was on a long ago Christmas Eve,
But then, somewhere he listed it as *mid-January?*
It was so long ago that you wouldn't even believe!
Guess he didn't know that birthdays are binary.

This raises a most interesting question or query,
What is Bud trying to hide or at least conceal?
(At the very time of year we're making merry!),
Preventing his friends from making it a big deal!

I'm guessing the older he gets the more he abides it,
Why would anyone NOT want to celebrate his birth?
Cause when you ask, he starts to hedge and hide it.
Just because he likely gained a few pounds of girth?

It took me many years to teach him how to read texts!
And you might just as well forget about *Messenger,*
Teaching him how to respond to those comes next.
That will require diplomacy, *ala,* Henry Kessinger!

Anyway Bud, at the possible risk of sounding silly,
I think that covers it! There's not much left to say!
Except,
Play something like, *Turn Out The Lights*, by Willie!
And have a wonderful and great belated birthday!

And even though *The Party's almost Over*
Grab your hearing aid and glasses and false teeth,

And pretend you're young enough to play *Red Rover*,
And that you're still age 40 or somewhere underneath,
Or,
About the age of this year's 2021 Christmas wreath!
Which, of course is…sadly… a false belief!
Written on December 26, 2021
for my *"old"* friend, Bud Farrar, 82nd Birthday…on Christmas Eve.

Consider the Lilies!
(Happy 84th Birthday, Tim!)

Tim, It almost brings me to tears,
When I calculate both <u>our</u> lives in yards!
But to cover the sum total of <u>your</u> years,
Count them! I had to buy three cards!
At the Dollar Tree!
And they ain't free!
I'm just hoping I never catch up to you, Timothy!
Both our days are numbered, my friend,
But 15 days more seems like a decade or two,
The closer one comes to the end!
So,
Put on some mellow music and dance.
Carpe Diem! This *Mid-January* day is yours!
For birthdays were made for love and romance.
But only after you eat your *soupe du jours,*
Is it legit to *chug-a-lug* another Coors!
Now!
I'm pretty sure, Tim, I will go before you do,
And reap my final reward, from Him!
For it will take our Lord a bit longer to build,
That *Welcome Home Mansion,*
In the midst of *The Lilies of the Field,*
Which He's building for Kersti and Tim!
So that,

The two of them, can be with Him!
Just to sit in His presence and chat!
Now,
Consider that!
For Timothy Stoen's birthday, January 16, 2022

Timothy Stoen, Deputy District Attorney
Photo Credit, Don Claybrook, Sr.

Gig 'Em!

There's a farm-boy/military school yonder in south-central Texas,
Not in California; but, in the homeland of three of my three exes.
They play football supported by that silly infamous _Twelfth-Man_.
Very good at yelling, but at football? Somewhat of an _"also-ran._

Who ran, you ask? That's a good question for old Texas A&M.
The cadet corps came to that school on little more than a whim.
Praised by the alumnae whose heads were covered with baggies,
They enrolled and became the brunt of all jokes....those Aggies!

Not to worry, the ubiquitous <u>Aggie Joke</u> is their claim to fame.
They embrace and cherish those, far more than that silly game.
Should you ask them what caused them to arrive at such a day,
They'd just look as if they hadn't a clue...cows puzzled by hay.

I recall a game twixt _That Good Old Baylor Line_ and A &M.
This writer was ejected for displaying too much vigor and vim,
Remembering that football game twixt the Aggies and Baylor,
While kicking, screaming and hissing, like a half-drunk sailor.

Two men go into a public restroom, both of them needing badly to pee.
The Aggie washes his hands, The Baylor man's zipper goes _zippity zee._
Cadet: _"We're taught to wash our hands, following this kind of relief."_
Bear: _"We're taught not to pee on our hands. That's our Baptist belief."_

If you're an Aggie, that's ok, never deny it. It's your heritage.
I suppose upon reflection, it might just have a bit of _merit-age._
Aggies serve a very good purpose when all things one invokes.
If it weren't for those farmers, we'd have no more Aggie Jokes!
<u>May 14, 2018</u>

It Takes Two to Tango!

Happy birthday…Jeannie, my very special friend.
We'll not talk about which number this birthday is,
Neither the middle nor the end…just another bend.
And God's truth be told…it's really nobody's biz!

Maybe we should post a couple of armed guards,
Because, Jeannie, I want to allay all your fears,
I had to *cut-to-the-chase*, and purchase two cards,
Just to cover the sum total of your wonderful years.

As old Will said…*"That's the unkindest cut of all."*
The summer years wane…slowly turning to fall.
My advice? Go spend $Big $Bucks at the mall!
That's all!
P.S. Now, put on some music and dance!
Birthdays were meant for romance,
For Jeannie and Brandt, per chance.
But make it a waltz, appropriate for a Southern Belle,
And not,
A Tango, by Latin Lover, Carlos Gardel.*
*Nope! You'll have to Google it!" October 6, 2020 for Jeannie's Birthday!

April 12, 2019
8:42 PM

TIME STAMP

Tribute to a Traveler!
Autumn Claire on her trip to Everest! Photo Credit: Someone to whom she handed her iPhone!

Marvelous Lonely Hearts' Club!

We meet on third Fridays, and generally about every third month,
Or months that start with "J,"
With the best view in Mendocino, the home of our charming hostess,
The diminutive Darlene Clay!

But we miss JoAn…and Jim and Laurel, that handsome Hunter duo,
Each left us with a tear,
And who could forget Betty Freeman, and Delightful Daphne' Beard?
Both added a chunk of cheer!

But life goes on with Ann Fischer, Barbara Foote and Tamara Fites!
``Two ladies…and a Kid named *"Trouble!"*
And another poet in the room, the irrepressible and witty Judy Sinclair.
She could be my double!

Then there's my beautiful and lovely fellow Bear, Patricia Lacey!
Our Alma Mater is Baylor!
While Capt. Matt Leach adds a touch of swagger, and lots of dash,
Like a witty drunken sailor.

If the real poet, Elizabeth Kirkpat…*What's-her-name,* with *panache,*
And a smidgen of snap,
Will behave herself, be nice and sweet, and remember who she is,
I might let her sit in my lap!

Jan Wallace recently had knee surgery and is back doing quite well.
I mean she's on the mend.
But I saved the very best for last, because it's my method of madness,
As this sad tale comes to an end.

The two Dons in the room, Scheffel and Claybrook, are witnesses,
Who not only listen but loom,
And are present as a guarantee…that without any reasonable doubt,
There…will…be… an… adults… in… the…room!

Even as our *Lonely Hearts Club…*gaslights in the gloom.
Written for the get-together of our singles' group, Friday, June, 17, 2022
Don Claybrook, Sr. June 15, 2022.

Martha Lee!

I want you to meet a friend of mine,
From Stephenville Texas, a town so fine.
I haven't really known her for long,
But she has my heart singing a song.
Stephenville *(and her pretty face)* on Facebook,
Caused me to take a long second look.
So with trepidation, I introduced myself to her,
And every day since then has been a blur.

The days passed by and the nights did too,
And our messages on Messenger fairly flew.
We've talked about everything from soup to nuts,
And like Dandy Don, even *"ifs" and "buts!"*

Now I'm a pretty good judge of weather and people,
Can read them both like the sky does a steeple.

She just as nice as she can be,
She's a friend of mine. She's Martha Lee!
It seems that my Lord has answered my prayer,
But it remains to be seen if there's a *"there"* there!
November 21, 2019

My Father's Voice!

I loved to hear my daddy's voice
Day's end when work was done.
But these few words were always choice,
"Looks nice, good job, my son."
*

But now as dark gives way to light,
I hear a higher call.
"It's time once more to bless the night."
"Awake, Arise, Stand Tall."
1995-96

My Replacement!

The heart of a Texan
The soul of a poet
The mind of a genius
(Oh, yes, we all know it.)
A minister, a lawyer, A Christian, a man,
But most of all
A football fan

Cathy Rowbottom, February 18, 2022
See also on this Book's back cover!

Our Junior Miss!

D.J.
Had another little Sis,
God sent her, like a gentle kiss.
She brought much bliss,
She's quite a pearl,
Our Junior Miss,
What a girl!
April 11, 2019

Rhymes and Phases!

A good friend is for always.
Not just the bright and sunny days!
Nor happy ways.
But for bad rhymes,
And the every phase,
Of hard times.

The Branded Man!
(Brandt Stickel's 70-Something Birthday)

Well, it's March 14th, Monday. Today we celebrate Bran!
But the Bran we celebrate today, is a lawyer man!
Not,
Pieces of grain husk separated from flour at the mill.
Bran with a small **"d"** added, if you will.
Making a brand on which we all can stand!
However,
Something's amiss! We still need a Tee.
Just a plain old ordinary **"t"** don't you see?
Not what you place under your golf ball!
If we're to celebrate before Summer? Or perhaps even Fall.
What we need is a lower case **"t"** to have at our *beck and call!*
And so,
I do believe we're maybe making some real progress on this,
But surely you didn't think it was all gonna be bliss?
When ya got Don, blended with bad weather?
(A bad mix for anchoring a feather!)
Or anything else!
Trying to celebrate when all the pieces are together!
Finally,
Just put the lower case **"d"** & the **"t"** on his,
And remember, as you're reading this, there will be a quiz!
Then up and add all that to the *grain-less* Bran!
While you're *de-corking* a bottle, for a Champaign fizz!

Because my masterpiece is my way of wishing,
Brandt a Happy Birthday!
On this special day of his!
*
From Don Claybrook, Sr.
Better known, *(If it's anybody's biz),*
As The Poem Writing Whiz!
(Who needs Champaign for fizz?)
P.S.
If God can change a man's name from Didymus to Thomas,
(And the Lord did a real favor for old Tom when He did!),
And another man's name, from Saul to Paul,
Then like Thomas, I've got my doubts, if He cares if I change,
A grain called Bran, to Brandt!
Creating the large from the small.
Because,
It is the *Birthday Boy's* name, after all!
February 24, 2022 for your birthday, March 14, 2022!

The Legend of Richard Eldon Suggs!
(My Brother-in-law!)

Our Lord is good and faithful, and loves us much more,
Than words can capture.
He delivered Richard from cancer and death, a deliverance,
Not unlike the rapture.
Rudyard Kipling said it best...Richard had met both,
Triumph and disaster,
Defeating both imposters, and now loving life again, and at home,
In the presence of his Master.
Richard had a very full life, except for these last 19 years,
Of Evil's very bad curse,
While living in the arms and love of Lanora, his joy, his life,
And yes, his nurse.
So Rick, Des, and KJ, you were given the very best,

That our Lord has to offer.
A mother and father who loved you unconditionally.
They gave you all that life can proffer.

So now my tribute to this good man ends with,
"We'll join you Richard, where love does abound.
In the morning, or perhaps at noon; or, when the
Setting sun goes down."

The rest of Richard's story is best written,
As a man who could work miracles,
With simply kind words and hugs.
The remarkable life of a very good man,
The legend of Richard Eldon Suggs.
January 8, 2018

The Legend of Timothy Stoen!
(See photo on 109)

It was in the year of our Lord, *nineteen-hundred and thirty-eight,*
On a winter's day in January. Good grief! What a cold, hard fate!
When a bouncing baby boy entered into the Stoen's family nest.
And Mom and Dad Stoen, knew that they'd been divinely blessed.

His mother was a good Presbyterian. Calvinist all the way through.
Tim told me his dad was something else. What? I haven't a clue.
Young Master Stoen grew up, and he lived his life as an Indian's arrow,
That is, he learned to walk in his Christian faith, sure, straight and narrow.

Timothy was as sharp as the proverbial tack. That was so very clear.
He mesmerized his mom and dad, like headlights mesmerize a deer.
School had to be a piece of cake for young Timmy, though he might deny,
And say that he worked his backside off, while dreaming of pie in the sky.

The years just passed right on by, like days and years are won't to do.
Tim was making his mark in the world; but, a storm was about to brew.
Because our idealistic lad dreamed of a world where everyone was equal,
A place and time, a state of mind, where there was no model nor prequel.
Passion was life and life became his passion, indistinguishable it seems.
Perhaps that's why old men have visions and young men dream dreams.
Napoleon met his Waterloo; and, young Tim was about to meet his curse.
The General was banished to a rock called Elba; Tim's fate was worse.

He did what he could for the cause, a mouthpiece for Jim Jones I suppose.
And drifted with the tide of evil's ruthless design; but, who really knows?
He heard his Lord's call, *"Come out from among them! Do so this day!"*
And Tim, just like the swallows returning to Capistrano, did so sans delay.

Our Lord is very faithful and loves us much more that words can capture.
Tim was delivered from *"The Devil of Jonestown,"* not unlike the rapture.
And Rudyard Kipling said it best, Tim had beat both triumph and disaster,
Defeating both imposters; and now, he was serving a different Master.

So now my tribute to this good man...ends with *"We'll miss you Tim,"*
As Colorado awaits you and Kersti, beyond the Continental Divide's rim.
I'll not tease you as I usually do; although, I did have that kind of whim.
And now you know the rest of the story, the one for whom love did atone,
The remarkable life of a godly man, The Legend of Timothy Stoen.
<u>With love and appreciation for your being an extraordinary man and friend, Tim!</u>

The 2019 Lady Bears!

Let me introduce you to the 2019 Lady Bears.
This Terrific Team comes in *half-a-dozen* pairs,
With Coach Kim Mulkey cracking her whip,
These ladies are playing like a block off the chip.

Now our number 1 is a lot like the Mona Lisa,
With that enigmatic smile adorning our NaLyssa.
She's as smooth as silk, and that's no myth,
Our lass from Converse, that's NaLyssa Smith!

Our numbers are not ranks, but #2 is speedy,
Quite the defender is Richards, first name DiDi.
She comes between Smith and #3 Trinity.
I could go on about this duo beyond infinity.

Trinity Oliver, what a beautiful name, I missed,
Not a common name Trinity; but, Oliver's a Twist.
Our gal from Euless Texas, Trinity, is *three-in-one*.
Score, defend and assist…her game's a lot of fun!

Now number 4 is a lady called *Scott-Grayson*,
She's as Honest as a 35th degree Catholic Mason!
That's cause she went to Riverside <u>*Baptist*</u> High,
N.J. That'll make you *throw-up* a brick and cry.

Well now, our number 10 is Aguira DeCosta,
Who's neither from Atlanta nor even Valdosta.
Waco is *brand-new* to this Sacramento lass.
But California is golden, so let's give her a pass.

Would you believe that #12 is a girl named Moon Ursin?
She came from Louisiana just blessin and cursin.
This drummer plays basketball in a different tune,
With this Miss Ursin, Baylor's hung the Moon!

What do you do when you have all these?
You recruit Lauren who's taller than most trees.
Our #15 was born making stops and blocks,
And a *poster-maker's* dream, is our Miss Cox.

But nobody's crazier than Texas' own Gary Busey.
And nobody shoots threes like our Texas gal Juicy!
From right there in Waco comes our Lady Landrum.
If they shoot like her, just catch 'em and brand 'em.

How in the world does one replace Carson, aka, Johnny?
Just bring her in and announce, "Heeerrrssss Kalani!
She's from Slidell Louisiana, and she has no crown,
But she's surely a queen like Egbo, our Miss Brown!

Jackson was a forward young lady, but got the point,
When Coach Kim Mulkey did this LSU grad anoint.
She's all business without being flashy and showy.
Our gal from Maryland, just call her Sweet Chloe.

Now, speaking of Egbo, Baylor's erstwhile queen,
Is like singing a sonnet 'bout a basketball machine.
She's from Travis High in old *Houston -Town,*
We sure are happy to have this Queen around!

That leaves just one more, her name's Bickle.
She's the kind of lady who make men fickle.
Caitlin is number 51 in your program, 'tis true.
But in your heart, she's a dream come true.

Well, that's our 2019 Lady Bears' basketball team.
They've put a smile on our face, given us reasons to dream,
Of Sweet 16's, Elite 8's and final 4's!
When Baylor Bears dream, it doesn't rain, it pours.
The 2019 Season ended with the Lady Bears winning the National Championship!

The 2021 Baylor Men's National Basketball Championship!
Just two years after the Lady Bears won their third
Basketball National Championship, the men won their first!

Twenty-Twenty-One!

The Baylor Men, not to be outdone,
Just two years after the Lady Bears won,
Won one too!
Now if that won one too,
Sounds like a palindrome to you,
It's likely true, if the game was on played on 12/2/21.
It's part of March Madness, they say,
So likely the Bears won it in April!
But, as long as that tourney goes today,
Hey! What I can say,
It could have been May!
But they won it all…anyway!
Never mind which day!
February 7, 2022

Tinker Toys and Fiddlesticks!

Tweedledee and Tweedledum,
Very low and oh so glum.
Kind of lonely, awfully blue,
Many dark colors …A sad hue.

Doctor checked me out real good.
Said my heart was made of wood.
But…like a hammer hits a nail,
Thought he knew what made me ail.

Gave me a script---nothing complex,
A smile with all its side-effects.
And offered lots of sage advice,
Something about *"Men and Mice."*

Now my mood was on the rise..
What had caused this nice surprise?

Well, Tinker Toys and Fiddlesticks!
All I needed was a *"Stickel Fix."*
June 18, 2017
See the Preface to this book for a note about this poem.

Uncle Dave!

I realize now, Uncle Dave was my boyhood hero, as I look back,
He was like a big *eight-wheeler*, running down the railroad track.
He was carefree and unmarried. Nothing could stop Uncle Dave!
Doing *"his thing,"* caused some to question, his desire, to behave.

He quite often took Stan and me walking, and hunting or fishing,
Crossing railroad tracks, with our small cane poles just a 'swishing,
Coming home just about dusk, was like being on a permanent leave.
But Uncle Dave was bound by nothing; clocks were his *pet-peeve*.

Being a Claybrook, nobody told him what to do, he was one of a kind,
Stubborn as the proverbial mule; no patience with those who whined.
On those lazy, hazy summer days, cares of the world were miles away.
Being with Uncle Dave was our joy, shunning work, we chose to play.

He was his very own man, having nothing at all, not ever even a wife.
Made sense to Stan and me. If given a choice, we'd rather have a knife.
No woman to hold him down, no steady job, where every day he went.
He usually lived with us, or another relative, Never had to pay rent.

Dad was a plumber, Uncle Dave's baby brother, Dad always had his back.
But they would go to war with each other, neither of them giving a jack.
Blood is thicker than water, they say, except when tempers come to blows,
Sadly, those two blood brothers, both lost, when friends became foes.

Uncle Dave joined the army, back in the Stone Age, during World War I,
Wanting to win the war for democracy, a promise made; but never done.
When my uncle saw the writing on the wall, he applied for a *3-day leave*.
When Uncle Sam granted it, my uncle left. He, they would never retrieve.

He departed from the Philippines. How? Perhaps we will never know.
Years later he filed to sue Uncle Sam for back pay, a whole lot of dough!
He was likely drinking beer when he *"filed."* I'm guessing he was full.
His imagination was not thinking *"legal."* He was actually full of bull!

He lived with us on the Gulf Coast and slept in the same bed as Stan and I.
One night he came home wearing his left shoulder on his right eye!
The heat and humidity conspired. Uncle Dave was speaking his mind,
"This heat box!" He crumpled on my body, his verbiage not refined.

I was a grown with wife and children when Uncle D. passed in Oklahoma.
They said he died as stubbornly as he lived, and passed while in a coma.
The preacher spoke as if my uncle were a saint! We knew better than that;
So we prayed for God's grace, as he stepped up, for his very last *at-bat.*

After all these years I've had time to reflect on all the vile things they said,
"He was a no good son of a B;" or, *"We're all better off with him dead."*
My mind drifts back to those summer days of fishing, hunting, all so fine,
I choose the beginning rather than the end, as I come to the end of the line.
I know not what course others may take; or how that might opine,
But…Uncle Dave will always be remembered…as a friend of mine.
<u>Written August 2, 2017, with a thankful heart for my Uncle Dave.</u>

<u>We Be Styling!</u>

Looking good in the Hood,
Like I knew you would!
Stepping up a notch,
As there you stood!
Wearing your Apple watch,
<u>In your *fleece-lined hood!*</u>
Upon sending my friend, Jeannie, an ad advertising
Apple watches, with a matching hooded jacket.
<u>Monday, Oct. 11, 2021.</u>

Mendocino Baptist Church
Photo Credit, Don Claybrook, Sr.

Whatsoever Things!

Sixty-eight years of wedded bliss,
Sixty-eight years of foolidge.
Sixty-eight years since a lass named Stewart
Married a young man named Coolidge.

Twenty-four thousand, eight hundred and twenty,
Now that's a lot of days!
Seventeen more for years that leap,
In a hundred different ways.

Twenty-four thousand, eight hundred thirty-seven,
They've moved a lot of freight.
He's preached 10,000 time or more.
She's never once been late.

"I'll decide all the big things," Dick told her,
"And you decide the little."
She's always agreed with that enigmatic smile,
And he was left to unravel the riddle!
As he played *second-fiddle!*
(apparently ALL their decisions were little)

And down through all those wonderful years,
Dick said they had no major collisions,
And basically lived with few real fears,
Because Charlotte made ALL the decisions

Back on that day, she said, *"I do,"*
And he said, *"I do too."*
Their whatsoever days they spent
On whatsoever things are true.

And on this most special night,
Twenty-four thousand, eight hundred thirty-seven,
Keep on doing the *"Whatsoever Things,"*
And embrace your foretaste of heaven.
*

**On the occasion of Dick and Charlotte Coolidge's
68th wedding anniversary,
<u>June 12, 2006</u>**

So, we come to the end of another chapter, and what do I feel? I feel a sadness that the only way most of the folks to whom I've paid tribute in this category, will ever be noticed in any other way. Not all, because some have. For those who haven't, I honor with this set of poems. Our Lord knows you quite well…

April 29, 2020 10:43 AM

Mendocino County Line
By Don Claybrook, Sr. on the date shown!

CHAPTER 7
Poems about,

PLACES

And Life Got in My Way!

Born when my world had gone to hell, because of The Great Depression,
Old Will Rogers had his favorite target, Congress, meeting in extra session.
FDR had saved the day with names like CCC, REA and the good old WPA.
There was not yet a chicken in every pot; however, soup lines had gone away.
But now, *"We've Got the Devil to Pay"* was regretfully a slogan here to stay,
In Graham Texas!
We didn't owe the Devil a single cent. That was spent when the veil was rent.
Times were getting better; but, life was still awfully hard in Graham, Texas.
There in '38 when we ignorantly thought there were still two different sexes.
Ten years 'ere Mr. Kinsey in '48, when we learned our *gender-neutral* fate.
But the world kept on its appointed rounds; and, we just fished or cut bait,
In Graham Texas!
The little town of Graham was perhaps best noted for its courthouse square;
The poor working souls who spent their *"fortunes"* while passing time there.
Nobody yet knew nor dreamed of that geometrical figure; but all the same,
Names like *"square"* had not yet infiltrated the *ever-changing* name-game
In Graham Texas!
Life was indeed simple, with always just enough time to be a neighbor.
Visiting with our fellowman was not a bad thing, rather a love, not a labor.
Not just to have one; but, to be one. No need in our town for good fences.
Where country folks come to chat; and, where true friendship commences,
In Graham Texas!
I grew up loving life, and the air I breathed, and Buster, my faithful dog,
And a pig dad found for me; but alas! Curly grew up and became a hog.
Life was about to teach me about parting ways, and the ways of who I am,
I learned that the sorrow of giving up Curly, would lead to the love of ham,
In Graham Texas!
But time did pass; and, in forty days and forty nights, I became a man,
And that I knew beyond a reasonable doubt that my Lord had a plan.
A design for my life that would let Love come in and with me abide,
A calling that couldn't be ignored; nor, could it be set aside, or denied,
In Dallas Texas!
I studied and applied myself. I would be a preacher, *God-called* for sure,

And become the prophet my Lord wanted me to be, brave honest and pure.
But something happened to that dream. I know not what. It's hard to say.
I left Graham, Texas, with the wonder of a *big-eyed* boy, I'd show the
Devil who had to pay.
But that's when the bridge began to sway,
And life got in my way.
In Beaumont Texas.
Don Claybrook, Sr. January 15 in what year I know not!
In honor of another preacher and prophet on his birthday, Dr. Martin Luther King, Jr.

Anointed One!

New Life On Strawberry Point,
His Chosen One He did anoint,
And did appoint,
To walk the way,
From Sin's disjoint,
By the Bay!

A Promise to Keep!

We'll leave on Thursday when kids take flight,
Drive all day, then spend all night,
At Holiday Inn in old Eugene;
Breathe fresh air and vent our spleen.

Now Friday morning will find us going,
But by nightfall, we'll be slowing.
Hot on the trail like J. Edgar Hoover.
Ho-Jo's waiting in big Vancouver.

Saturday's arrival in Alberta Land,
A likely place to take our stand.
Three nights in a row, I'll hold my *"squeeze,"*
And soak up heaven in Lake Louise.

On the road with Willie and Charlie again,
Making more than music with my friend.
It's already Tuesday, low on loot,
The best, Best Western is waiting in Butte.

Up on Wednesday and heading south,
Pocatello, Idaho! Well shut my mouth!
Come dark again, because it fits my ditty,
The Radisson is waiting in Salt Lake City.

Thursday finds us heading west,
Doing that which we do best.
Loving life and loving to roam,
Loving to wander, but heading home.

With Reno or Tahoe somewhere between,
And if we still have a little green.
No more expecting a big dump truck,
It's Charlie's time for a little luck.
Maybe on Friday; Not as late as Sunday.
In maybe a Caddy; or, maybe a Hyundai.
We've made the circle, enjoyed the thrills,
Home again and happy as El
In El Dorado Hills.
Summer of 1992

Back Home Again!

Back home in Texas again,
Three exes would become just friends.
Where would it end ?
But I was back.
A recycled trend,
And,
<u>That's a fact.</u>

Cloud on the Mountain!
Mt. Rainier! Photo taken by my daughter, Claire (Claybrook) Kriofske, November 22, 2021
58 years to the day after the assassination of JFK!

<u>Behind and Basking!</u>

Bills are mounting, and so are the riders;
Both of them beg to be paid.
Bettors are betting on old *one-nighters*
As both are beginning to fade.
Out of the night come doubts and despair,
Out of the day comes a tear.
"Out of this world, what a lovely pair!"
With nothing to fear but fear.

Now I lay me down to sleep,
There's nothing to do but wait.
No appointments at all to keep.
Early is quite often too late.

So, I'll go on my way and the world will ask,
"What did he have to say?"
"If you want to finish September's task,
You'd better start in May."

Now if you think I've lost it all,
Since I'm way behind on my bills,
There's nowhere on earth, I'd rather stall,
Than in El Dorado Hills.
October 26, 1992

Blue Grass and Basketball!

The blue grass state was next up,
Churchill Downs and the governor's cup,
And Adolf Rupp!
Basketball and rings,
Derbies and things!
Five years abrupt,
Bottom of the cup.
<u>Fat lady sings!</u>

Bound For the Land!

We left Texas bound for the Land,
Of the Sacramento,
Off we'd go, kids in tow,
Rolling with the flow.
Could we forget?
What He'd know!

Place your bet.
<u>Win, place or show?</u>

Coast With the Most!

July! Time to beat the heat,
Time to put sandals on your feet,
And cop a beat.
Stay on the Coast,
But don't you cheat!
Just pose a toast.
And
Take a seat!
<u>July 1, 2021</u>

Five Aces!

Texas is really five states,
With five different kinds of fates.
Fences she hates!
Open spaces,
Do not need gates,
Nor basis.
Just kick off the traces!
And call Texas *Home*
Or at least, an Oasis!
Where you'll never more roam!
<u>2018</u>

Happy Texas!

Well, old Happy Texas isn't very happy anymore.
Downtown there's now a padlock on every door.
The Ogallala Aquifer, after a million years, ran dry.
And folks pray for rain, but the sky refuses to cry.

In the 40's and 50's, they drilled holes everywhere.
The pumps brought water, some here, some there,
To assuage the thirst of crops famished by drought.
Now the folks ask, *"What's this outcry all about?"*

Plains cowboys labeled the stream, *"Happy Draw!"*
But the depletion of the Ogallala was the last straw,
And that's how this blissful little town got its name.
The drought of 2012 ushered in a *brand-new* game.

Experts say it will take only a few million plus years,
So, think again of the people…and their many fears,
And the Ogallala Aquifer will replenish itself sublime.
So, say a prayer for them, without reason or rhyme,
Let's recall a town named Happy, a very sweet place,
With the old Ogallala Aquifer gone without a trace.
So, think again of the people…and their many fears,
And bend an arm while toasting with Lone Star beers,
To the aquifer that once defined it,
Now known simply as,
"The Forgotten Stream of Tears!"
May 12, 2020

Life on Strawberry Point!

New life on Strawberry Point,
He chosen one he did anoint,
And did appoint,
To walk The Way,
From sin's disjoint,
By The Bay

Mendocino!

From below the rivers and beyond the stars,
Where silt and eagles go.
Come murky memories of soaring flights,
And rushings to and fro.

The whirlwind twisted, the fire enlisted,
All who would see the show.
But the wind did wane, the fire refrain,
To a tiny ember-glow.

All was gone and near forgotten,
Like footprints in the snow.
What might have been was just a dream,
Where angels fear to go.

Nothing was left but the past to ponder,
Not even the prophet could know.
But a still small voice would whisper,
Again,
"Mendocino!"
November 16, 1995

Mendocino Mystique!

And my favorite critique,
On the Mendocino Mystique,
Is really chic.
Hip to the bone,
Not for the meek,
But the strong.
1996

Mendocino on My Mind!

Mendocino's Mystique is beyond knowing, but the mystery?…It's real,
Evoking magical days and nights…when our hearts, and time stood still.
Mine beats a beat faster, when I approach, the *Mendocino County Line.*
Mendocino!… Just the very name, beckons stardust memories of mine.

I cherish each precious moment, I spent in that small village, so quaint,
But to ever discern what its secret is, would begin and end with *"shan't."*
A cliff on the Pacific, blue skies, a hamlet, its *"Hollywood-North"* fame?
No! The wonder of our *"Paradise Found,"* Mendocino! Is simply in its name.

So, if you're ever in our neighborhood, and yearn to experience a unique place,
Find the Magic of Mendo! Kissed by God, and his incredible Amazing Grace.
Where the Pacific gets lost in its ebb and flow, you'll arrive, and you too will find,
Our hauntingly mystical hamlet, leaving as I do, with Mendocino on Your Mind.
Monday, July 10, 2017

Mendocino Time!

Mendocino is breathtaking, even when not at its best,
Edenic, even when hosting, the most cynical guest.
They all march to Eden, thinking everyone will win.
Forgetting, Paradise was lost, because of Original Sin,
Marching to Eden, On Mendocino Time.

Life settles down in time's unique gait, to a very slow pace,
But oftentimes, someone will refuse to even get into the race.
Very few understand, it's better to run, to simply compete,
For to do nothing at all…always ends in total, utter defeat,
While running, On Mendocino Time.

And when their days are long gone, and it's time to leave,
Our guests reluctantly depart, they've been given a reprieve,
From the mad hustle and bustle, without reason or rhyme,
Leaving with empty pockets, save perhaps, one thin dime!
Spending life on Mendocino Time.

Mendocino, you're my friend, my sweetheart, my way to roll,
I've given you my broken heart. You've given me your soul.
I'll be forever grateful to the Lord above, you came my way,
Even with your *Mendocino-Mystique,* I've had so little to pay,
Except to give the Devil his due!
And that…..On Mendocino Time…..too.
July 13, 2017

No Pleasure in Paradise!

I've got to come up with $1,623 dollar's for March's bills,
Much of it going to *PG&E* for that fire at *Pleasure!*
On a fixed income of like $1,598, no added frills.
Treating my payment like a hidden treasure!
I'll quit Metoprolol, one of my BP meds,
And get 'em paid, but at my Leisure,
While sending the rest to the Feds,
As they take this man's measure!
Gov. Newsom sends me food,
And that helps a lot.
But I can't eat it all,
Thus, much of it goes to rot!
I could save, like a nickel or a dime,
And lose a few pounds around the waist.
But getting a guitar to sound like a chime,
Ain't just a simply matter of *copy-cut-and-paste.*
So, I'll just keep paying the rent and juggling the rest,
And praying for the good Lord to provide for my needs,
While doing my dead-level best, as my sad life goes to seeds!
Now if anyone ever wants to tell me, *"Thank you,"*
For paying *PG&E's* bills, I'll just simply say,
"Oh, I didn't do it to be cherished or nice,
Nor for the Pleasure it gives to pay.
I just happily rolled those dice,
And did it for the good folks,
Who perished in
Paradise!
That day!"
March 9, 2021

School!

What is school?
School is brick, mortar, iron, glass, tile, wood and paint.
School is all this blended together in a proportion that makes
It easy to see, hear, write, study and think.
School is a monument…standing majestic on a green city block.
School is where the school bus stops to deliver its parcel.
School is silent serenity and boiling bedlam.
School is red, white, green, blue and yellow, all blended into
One noisy, ranting rainbow.
School is an escape from home and a sigh from mom.
School is a PE class where lost articles should get the grade.
School is the ABC's and the PTA's.
School is a haven for evolving scientists…all mad.

School is an incubator and percolator and a testament.
School is success; school is failure.
Yes, school is all these things; and yet, school is more.
School is a mass of crying, laughing, losing, winning, living,
Dying flesh and blood known as youth.

School is a good morning and so long and have a good weekend.
School is a parent who expects an A from a C head and
Usually gets a C from an A head.
School is room 12; or 6, or 8; or the visual aid's room.

School is the cafeteria that has begun to use cookbooks.
School is the wicked, evil, *never-smiling* beast, the teacher.
School is the grumpy librarian who has 10,000 books; yet,
Scares the student into leaving them be.
Bless her!
School is the principal and assistant principal who busy
Themselves with the absence reports and presence reports and the
Middle ground and marble dust.
School is the attendance secretary who is always present

Trying to find out why others are not.
Yes, school is all these, yet more…for school is tomorrow's
World, today…I pray.
First, written in the fall of 1963 and published in November issue of
<u>The Texas Outlook, official publication of the Texas State Teachers Association</u>

<u>Texas!</u>

Texas is a state of mind!
A special place for which man pined.
One of a kind!
Oh, to dream big
Time out of mind,
Heaven's gig.
<u>2018</u>

<u>Texas in My Rear-View Mirror!</u>

Texas again, frick and frack,
God on our side, we didn't lack.
We had the knack,
To get it done.
Had our back,
Gave his Son.
<u>2018</u>

<u>TEXAS! Living in a State of Grace!</u>

You'd lose your bottom dollar, if you think I don't bleed Dallas Cowboy Blue.
"How *'bout them Cowboys?"* It's our battle cry. The other teams haven't a clue.
My blood's not red, like the Redskins, Arizona or the San Francisco 49ers
That's our team out here in the Golden West, I just call them the *Forty-Whiners.*

They whine about odds and ends, especially when losing to *"America's Team."*
But, that's who we are, *"America's Team."* Just live with it. while you scream.

Dandy Don, Staubach, Aikman, Romo: A formidable quartet. Wait! Add Dak,
Named after a state. No wonder that the 40-Whiners, want Joe Montana back.

Montana v. Dakota; Joe v. Dak? We'd give away Joe and keep winning with Dak.
Or turn them every which way but loose, administering a *well-placed* whack!
But there's more going on in Texas than beating up on every team and their state.
In Texas, where cotton grows, the wind blows, and oil flows, we *fish or cut bait!*

I'm Texan by birth, a Californian by choice. What better place to sing my song?
I'd rather be outside throwing rocks at Texas, setting right what's gone wrong.
I can hear it now, all about glass houses and rocks and how dare you Don?
If a Texan is NOT lying to you a scrunch, he's being a dishonest con.

Folks not from Texas, have already added 50-points for the bragging Texans do.
So when the tall tales of Texans are over, there's nothing left to say but adieu.
Texas: the Cowboy buckle on the Bible Belt, where Baptists are a dime a dozen,
Everyone's been baptized a time or two, and your sister's probably your cousin.

Mom: *"Don't make me come over there. You know you always get the last word."*
Just like an honest to goodness Texan, I responded, *"Come on, that's absurd!"*
Texans love food, and have more restaurants which proclaim, *"All you can eat!"*
Than any place on the planet, where eating more than your buddy is quite a feat.

Knowing they'll need Weight Watchers, as they ponder, while eating S'mores,
The local Baptist Church will vote for their gymnasium to install *double-doors.*
Texans ain't the brightest bulb in the socket, for instance, take Bubba's sorry tale.
When the Texas Highway Patrol stopped him and asked if he wanted to go to jail.

The officer, doing his best, asked poor Bubba, *"Do you have any I.D. or not?"*
Bubba looked to his left and right, like a deer in a headlight asked, *"Bout what?"*
When I think of Texas, *I Remember the Alamo,* and that beautiful old *Lone Star,*
And get cold chills, like any Texan would, when visitors visit our state from afar.

I thank my God for life, liberty and happiness, for a state about which I can cry,
I'll sing the praises of the Lone Star State, and sing it with my head held high!
Texas our Texas all hail the mighty state. Texas our Texas, so wonderfully great!

Texans pride place, telling our children they live in a *state of grace*! That's fate.

In the seventh grade we had Texas history, the most moving history in the world,
And then we sang, *Texas our Texas*, while standing to honor our flag unfurled.
The Old Chisholm Trail's gone, blown away by Time, and the West Texas wind.
And the prairies Goodnight roamed, lost a bit of Texas and, a very good friend.

God has smiled on Texas. with our hole in the roof where the Cowboys play.
He can make a date to watch His favorite team…blow their opponent away!
Texas, I love you, I always will, no matter how long I'm gone or where I roam,
And, from New Mexico to Texarkana, from the Panhandle to the Gulf's foam,
From the Piney woods to the plains, the Gulf, and the rest of the state I bind.
Wherever I roam, whatever I've seen, *Texas…You were always on my mind*.
Written Monday, July 10, 2017

The Geriatric Shuffle!

I'm getting old, but I still get around like a young man.
From Fort Bragg, Stockton and Elk; but, not Pakistan,
And I get up and go where the sky and roads take me.
From Louisville to Laredo, Wounded Knee to Waikiki.

Corpus Christi, Lodi, San Antonio, Reno; but not Siam,
Waco, Mendocino, Flour Bluff have made me who I am.
Yon Sydney, the Great Barrier Reef and Mineral Wells,
And so many more of life's hills, rivers and happy trails.

Spent a spell in Beaumont Texas in The Golden Triangle,
Which all ended when my life became a hopeless fandangle.
Higher Education was in the textbooks for my middle two.
Upon arrival, I was beset by myriad choices. So, who knew?

And also, there's London, Paris, St. Petersburg and Madrid,
Wanted to do China, but the SARS epidemic soon got unhid.
And the White Cliffs of Dover; yet, I've never been to Nome.

I got my China rebate and it was good just to stay at home.
South America was wonderful! We did the ABC's. That trio,
Would be Argentina and Brazil, with Buenos Aires and Rio.
Ipanema and Copacabana were nice, but so was old Chile.
And the ubiquitous, but always delightful, *Hard Rock Café*.

Nor to Antarctica, land of the frozen tundra and polar bear.
You're like, *"Why didn't you Just say, 'I've been everywhere.'"*
That kind of barren wasteland is bound to simply amaze ya.
Good question; but, truth be told, I've never been to Asia.

I came so close when we were in Chile and Punto Arenas,
Down south and a few miles straight down from Uranus.
Down very near to Cape Horn and *the jumping-off -place*.
But, I was bound for Santiago, with a smile on my face.

Africa's quite likely my favorite to endure the test of time,
Sweetwater was sweet with its sugary namesake sublime.
Nairobi was a modern makeover of an old ancient tribe.
Missionaries, safaris and crocks. Catch the nascent vibe?

I've taken you on this grand tour with me in order to say,
*"Don't fool yourself thinking I've turned a new leaf today,
Slowing down, relaxing, and getting my feathers in a'ruffle,"*
I never intended to get so old, as to do the *Geriatric Shuffle!*
May 8, 2018, Kieran's 15th birthday.

Where Dreams Come True!

Beyond the rainbow's soft hue,
I yearn for dreams that still come true.
Loving, praising,
Hope lives anew,
Amazing Grace,
From beyond the blue!

God has blessed me to live in some of the most iconic towns in America. For starters, I was blessed to live in one of the towns in California which was planned from the ground up and on day-one, *El Dorado Hills* in the foothills just east of Sacramento. Back then it would often make the lists of the *Top 10 Most Desirable Places to Live in The USA!* And then the quaint but unforgettable village of *Mendocino*, in Northern California and on the Pacific Coast, but just a short drive to the magnificent Redwoods and the Avenue of the Giants. I cherish all the towns and cities which the Lord provided for me to live; but, these two, along with two others, my hometown of Graham Texas stands out; and, also Waco, where I took my University degree. I, among all men, am most Blessed!

Autumn Claire

Note the Ellipsis on her cheek! The photo was taken long before I dreamed of calling
My collection of poetry by the same name, *Love's Ellipsis!* I only discovered her Ellipsis after
I had settled on a name for this collection! Photo credit: A *"Selfie"* by Autumn Claire.

Chapter 8
PONDERING

Poems of,

Reflections on Life.

Ellipsis of Love!

I enjoy writing poetry, I do it for various reasons, but mostly just for fun.
I write poems for birthdays, for special days, for simply getting it done.
Written poems for my daughters…and written for any old wind that blew.
Done poems for yesterday, today and tomorrow. I've written quite a few.

Now, I ponder and prepare to write more verse, and do so on bended knee,
What I can write, not vain nor trite, neither *"maybe"* nor *"what might be."*
As I reflect upon what is, or what might have been, I'm visited by a Friend,
The Spirit softly breathes to me, *"Write about The Beginning and the End."*

That was enough to convince me. When I'd written of the people I love,
I had forgotten the most important One, the One who came from above.
I frequently tell Him how much I love Him, because He first loved me,
But I'd not written a poem to share with Him…all in a brand-new key.

Carefree as a boy and his dog on a summer's day, I, only twelve years old,
Just as lost as the pearl of the woman; or, the Prodigal who had left the fold.
All the world had to offer, tugged at my heart; but, I couldn't sleep at night.
As miserable as the man who built more barns. Something just wasn't right.

Oh, I had read that *God so loved the world that He sent His only Son*,
And that He was *The Way*, *The Truth* and *The Life*, ere time had begun.
But my sins, my doubts, my questions…had me almost going insane.
And rumor had it that the road to heaven was marked by a narrow lane.

Try as I might, I couldn't understand, why Jesus would take **MY** place!
Upon reflection, I know it's simply because I was part of the human race!
It's not God's will that any should perish, but that all should choose Life!
But rejecting that choice is to choose brokenness, heartbreak and strife.

I'd tried everything, yet nothing worked. That's when I uttered, *"I give up!"*
At that moment it happened…I heard Him say, *"Here, drink from My cup."*
Like a trusting child with a *child-like* faith, I drank, and my world stood still!
Without knowing…by faith, I'd been set free by the Cross of Calvary's Hill.

I'd been saved! I'd been *born-again!* I'd tasted new wine, joy without end!
You're now *Alpha and Omega,* my Lord, my Savior, my *"Forever Friend!"*
I love you Lord Jesus. Abide with me. You give my heart a heavenly glow!
You carried away my sin. I could never repay. There was NO *quid-pro-quo!*
And now when my heart is broken, and when my life is ripped apart,
I just give it all to Jesus, who heals me and gives me a *brand-new* start.
Placing it all in his *nail-scarred* hands…not having a reason nor rhyme,
He faithfully makes me whole again, through His healing hands of time.

God in Christ, reconciling the world to Himself because He loved us so.
And now I want to tell Him how thankful I am…He refused to let me go.
I bow and acknowledge Him, just as, at the cross, did the Roman guard,
I'll declare throughout the ages and for eternity:
That Jesus Christ is Lord!
Sometime in 2017

A Few of my Favorite Things!

I like poetry that rhymes,
It's like matching lyrics with chimes!
And sunny climes!
Saxophone stars,
And then sometimes,
Chasing pars!
March 21, 2019

A Hurting Place!

In my absolute desolation of spirit and mind,
I turned to *The Other* who was beckoning me home.
That was it! I just wanted to go home,
To the bosom of warmth, and life and love,
To be there again; or, perhaps for the very first time.

I would return to hearth and home,
To the arms of mercy and abundant grace.
And that's when I knew.
When I knew the darkness,
In the midst of the light.

Sadly, I didn't know where home was.
Could it be that I had never been there?
Perhaps.
My search for eternity was a search for home.
Therefore, I can infer from my ponderings,
This:
Heaven is the eternal search for home!
Written on February 1, 1985 in a faraway place.
Revised 32 years later, on Dec. 1, 2017

A Walk in the Park!

Everywhere I look is dark!
Ominous clouds so very stark.
A walk in the park
Will do no good
Just another lark
In my 'hood.
May 2, 2018

Black and White!

Gray is the shade of *no-man's* land,
Half black, half white, awfully bland.
If understanding light, is your goal,
Experience *"The dark night of the soul."*

Without the night, we would lose the stars,
Misplaced, like our *"nears"* and our *"fars."*

A simple gift, neither rhyme nor reason,
More than gray; colors for every season.

Where no color is, there's no light. Life dies.
And without light, there are no rainbow skies.
The norm becomes simply, white and black,
Rainbows won't be, the only thing we lack.

Because, when we despair, we let love die.
And death comes with little more than a sigh.
The new color then, is black and white,
With Truth taking, its very last flight.
July 11, 2017.

Boys To Men!

When a boy becomes a man,
He needs no one to hold his hand.
A place to land,
Is just enough!
So let him stand,
Or call his bluff!

Come What May!

I've even searched *"Lost and Found;"*
Nothing but darkness all around.
I'm heaven bound,
But spend this day,
Hearing the sound,
Of *"Come what may!"*
July 22, 201

Count the Cost!

I was a prisoner…and bound!
Then angels flew close to the ground.
I almost drowned,
As life's seas tossed.
But a cross found,
Heaven's cost!
August 10,2020

Crazy!

Crazy for being lonely,
Crazy for loving you only.
Rightly or wrongly,
Life's gone to pot;
Yet, hopefully,
Love has not!
July 22, 2019

Get A Clue!

Jump out of the pan and into the fire,
Or join a church and sing in the choir.
But don't get stuck in the muck and mire,
Because someday, right out of the blue,
The fates might conspire,
And give you a clue!
10/11/2019

God's Economic Plan!

The price went up when heaven came down,
And God became a man.
The cross a burden, the thorns a crown,

In God's economic plan.
So if you're looking to invest,
In power and wealth and fame,
Just trust in Him, forget the rest,
The Name above every Name.
In the late 80's

I Also Ran!

I hitched my wagon to a star.
My Lord was with me near and far.
No hero nor,
King for a day,
Far under par,
But I **DID** play!

January 2021!

Twenty-twenty! What a shame!
Still, I heard that Santa Clause came!
But, COVID's no game,
That's plain to see.
So, who's to blame?
You or me?
January 1, 20

Lost Forever!

Some years are lost forever,
Which we simply have to sever.
They were never
Meant just to stay,
Just
An endeavor,
Gone astray.

My Sad Day!

My gosh, what a day it was,
With naught up, not even a buzz!
When doesn't, does,
Is distant kin,
And a kissing cuz,
A *"has been."*
July 22, 2019

My Search for Eternity!
(On turning forty-seven)

My *forty-seventh* year was spent looking for eternity.
I searched in the most unlikely places…
A Kansas City Convention Center;
A hospital which became a mental ward;
I even searched Hell.
No eternity here, except for the memories,
Not many good.
Two score and seven? Perhaps only a bridge to *forty-eight;*
Or, maybe just a number in the midst of numbers.
Nothing special. Something to be forgotten.
No eternity here, except for memories,
Not many good.
I looked for eternity on a *stone-covered* hill,
As one was committed to the cold hard earth.
I spoke eternal words that were marked in time.
"Now" was gone forever, to be lost in the past.
No Eternity here, except for the memories,
Not many good.
I looked for eternity in time and space;
But time passed, and space was dark.
And I was alone and afraid.
Afraid because my time and my space were dreadful.

No eternity here, except for the memories,
Not many good.
My memories were shrouded in mystery.
I looked for a glimmering glow of light,
Anything that would keep hope alive.
When all hope is gone, the void becomes
A hurting place.
In my absolute desolation of spirit and mind,
I turned to *The Other* who was beckoning me home.
That was it! I just wanted to go home,
To the bosom of warmth, and life and love,
To be there again; or, perhaps for the very first time.
I would return to hearth and home,
To the arms of mercy and abundant grace.
And that's when I knew.
When I knew the darkness,
In the midst of the light.
Sadly, I didn't know where home was.
Could it be that I had never been there?
Perhaps!
My search for eternity was a search for home.
Therefore, I can infer from my ponderings,
This:
Heaven is the eternal search for home!
February 1, 1985 in a faraway place.
Revised 32 years later, on Dec. 1, 2017 when the final three stanzas were added

Nickels and Dimes!

It has been said many times,
Youth is wasted on bad rhymes,
And nickels and dimes.
Early years come,
Ringing life's chimes.
And,

That's the sum!
In all times.
2018

Not A Clue!

Things were good, the sky was baby blue.
The weather was perfect, but who knew?
Before the day was through,
I'd need a friend.
But they had no clue,
At the end.
Revised January 15, 2018

Poignant

Sun shining down on leftover rain,
Eternal fire bathing temporary time.
Taking it all in, I reflect.
But my observations change nothing…
Unless…..
Unless…..there really is a noise
When a tree falls in a wood unattended.
Then what I see is at least poignant,
Except, with the "g" left out.
Neither it nor the noisy tree
Make much difference.
April 13, 2006

Questions Galore!

What makes a poem take flight?
What distinguishes day and night?
Do bedbugs bite?
Now here's a hint,

Get it right,
Before hitting, *"sent."*
May 14, 2019

<u>Quiet Times!</u>

Quiet Times on Cypress Ridge,
An Echo Dot is my bridge.
Magnets on fridge,
Tell the story,
Of my small smidge,
Of love and glory.
**<u>P.S. By the way, the magnets on my fridge
hold favorite Scripture verses.</u>**

<u>Reflections On My Birthday!</u>
<u>(84 And Still Counting)</u>

I've been a long time getting there,
And have seen much along the way!
Yet miraculously I guess I kept my hair,
Because I comb <u>something</u> every day!
What more can I say?
OK?
I've been around the world too.
From Paris Texas to Paris France.
And I can sing a bit of *Song Sung Blue,*
But I never learned to dance!
Never really got the chance!
I'm a Baptist!
One shouldn't drink from that dancing cup,
Presbyterians might accuse you of making love,
While standing up!
I love my Baylor Bears and Dallas Cowboys,
My *alma mater* and the 'Boys from old Big D!

But I was saddened that I never got *Tinker-Toys,*
Even though with Santa I always made my plea.
But speaking of love,
Yes! Tis true, I've been in love a few times,
And I honestly believe that love never fails,
But then again, without a reason or a rhyme,
I had three marriages which went off the rails.
Two were good, but one was like rusty nails!
But,
Now I'm neither complaining nor whining,
Nor pointing fingers at even one wife.
I enjoy beautiful ladies and fine dining,
But never learned to use a butter knife.
My life has been full of that kind of strife!
Now,
The best thing that ever happened to me,
Was when I invited Jesus Christ to come and dine.
He did!!! And now I can clearly see,
Because when He came, he brought the wine,
And that has made the difference for me,
For eternity!
So,

I threw away the bottle! And that was fine,
But not before the bottle was empty,
For I have indulged deeply
Of love's sweetest wine!
Won't you also come and dine,
And be a friend of His…and mine?
And enjoy the company,
Of the tie that binds!
*

**Written on January 3, for the occasion of my
84th birthday, February 1, 2022.**

Reflections on Yesterday!

Down the road to yesterday,
Where memories ignore tomorrow,
I wrap my mind around thoughts that play,
On moments of joy and sorrow.
Was it so good to be so young?
So hopeful, so bold, so free?
Or did the ladder forget the rung,
And the Piper forget the fee?
I have no <u>answers</u>
on things that count,
I have no eyes to see,
I only know as tomorrows mount,
My thoughts are thinking me.
<u>Date unknown, perhaps 2010</u>

Somewhere Over the Rainbow!

Beyond the rainbow's soft hue,
I yearn for dreams that still come true.
Where love lives anew,
My hopes a'raising.
And grace does too.
Amazing!
<u>May 3, 2018</u>

The Call!

Preaching is my divine call,
Can do no other lest I fall.
And much like Paul's
Damascus Road!
Through it all
<u>I abode.</u>

The Call That Wasn't Made!

What happens when refs are bad,
And miss a call they should have had?
A hanging chad?
Head in a cloud?
That's so sad,
For crying out loud,
Just make the call! That's all!
March 30, 2021

The Coronavirus!

The coronavirus is real!
Guess you could say it's the real deal.
But it's time to chill,
Shelter in place,
Or dang near kill,
The human race!
May 22, 2020

The End of Life!
Old Blue Eyes

Blue eyes crying in the rain,
From bearing so much hurt and pain.
No sweet refrain,
For this old boy.
Not much to gain,
Ship ahoy!
April 28, 2019

The Last Alert!

The end comes and pain dies slow,
But leaving's not the only way to go!
We reap, we sew,
Our last alert.
And now we know,
Life's awful hurt!
Revised January 15, 2022

The Triumvirate!

Daniel's lions were immense,
And Balaam's ass had common sense.
Jonah was dense.
All pressed their cause.
T'was recompense,
Without laws!
April 22, 2019

When Things Go Bad!

It seems that when things go bad,
We just turn to a brand new fad.
Trash what we had,
And all that stuff.
You think that's sad?
Not enough!
February 4, 2020

When Things Go South!

"You're a dish!! I'm fond of you."
She heard, *"I wish you a *mond adeau."*
Now here's a clue!

Bottom line, friend.
Neither one'll do.
You can't win!
*Mond, a variation of mound (big!)
<u>**Modified May 1, 2020**</u>

<u>*Where Did Tomorrow Go?*</u>

Where did tomorrow go?
On which I dreamed my dreams.

Perhaps into a million yesterdays,
In a thousand forgotten streams.

Where did tomorrow go?
I thought t'would never come.
Like a greeting and a final farewell,
It passed from to, to from.

Where did tomorrow go?
They say, *"It never comes."*
In a heartbeat…gone forever,
Yesterday's distant drums.

Where did tomorrow go?
I search in vain to find.
Loosed and near forgotten,
Like so many ties that bind.

Where did tomorrow go?
With hopes up the sky.
Perhaps I'll never really know,
That *"sweet bye and bye."*

And if there is no tomorrow,

(And I think like the poet does).
How do I posit anything?
Maybe yesterday never was.

Where did tomorrow go?
Only a fool would say.
I only know in tomorrow's present,
I'll always have today.
Written way back when!

Where Was God?

Harvey! One thinks of a large bunny and Jimmy Stewart,
But Harvey was neither.
A *pre-autumn* shower; or, a gentle zephyr from off the Gulf,
But Harvey was neither.
Those of us who watched, we who observed from a safer distance,
We began to ponder life's eternal question.
Warm and comfortable in our waterproof homes, we simply watched.
But still we pondered the ultimate question.
The stories and images came from strange sounding places,
Like Beaumont and Orange,
From places not so familiar as perhaps L.A. or San Francisco,
Places like Katy and Port Arthur,
Not unlike Fort Bragg or Mendocino.
We watched and began to know the vicarious pains of something lost forever.
And, *"The Question"* kept haunting us.
Lives being saved; but, lives also being lost…those will never come back.
"The Question" begs to be answered.
And, so we shall.
Where was God in the midst of so much pain, suffering and sorrow?
The God who delivers,
The *All-knowing* God who knew us 'ere we were conceived?
Where was He? <u>Where…was…He?</u>
Our God was not in the Hurricane, nor was He in the wailing wind.

Nor was He in the fire.
But, if we listen very closely, we can hear Him speaking to us,
In a still, small voice.
I was there when that small black baby was rescued by courageous men,
Did you see the wonder and hope in her eyes?
There in the boat when an elderly man who had given up all expectation of rescue,
Was indeed rescued by the Coast Guard.
I was there.
When the cable was hoisted up with its gondola filled with beautiful life,
I was there.
When a man breathed his very last breath while saving a total stranger,
I was there.
Do you believe my forever promise? I will <u>never</u> leave you nor forsake you.
I AM HERE!
When people from California to New York, from North Dakota to Mexico,
Were doing random acts of kindness,
Simply because they were inspired by what they were seeing in Texas,
I was there also!
Because I <u>allowed</u> Harvey to happen, I gave you many opportunities.
People can hope because of you.
They can experience the ecstatic joy of giving,
And know the power of love.
And know, perhaps for the very first time,
That I Am and forevermore Shall Be.
<u>August 30, 2017</u>

<u>While Wishing For Molly Ivins</u>

Coronavirus, indeed!
The U.S. is going to seed.
Here's what we need,
Tammany Hall,
And old Boss Tweed.
Someone call!
Wait!

Does that sound right…holy Cow!
Wait! I think that's what we've got now!
I'll take a bow,
Give up my plaint,
R. Nixon now,
Looks like a Saint!
March 29, 2020

Y'all Sure Do Talk Funny!

Is it armoire, wardrobe or even chifforobe?
Does chifforobe rhyme with row or probe?
I checked with Google. They haven't a clue!
That's when it hit me! That only God knew!
But He's not talking…out there in the blue!

Is it a verb, envelope? Or a noun, envelope?
Negative or no, or as we say in Texas, *Nope*?
But some folks pronounce it ahhhnn-velope!
For that gang there's very little, if any, hope!
We might as well be doing the *Rope-a-Dope!*

It's *"down"* to go south, and *"up"* to go north,
We can't say <u>home and</u> without saying <u>hearth</u>!
Why is it bad when something *"goes south?"*
Californians call it drought but we call it drouth,
In Texas, that will get a man hit in the mouth.

You call the late meal *dinner* and we call it *supper.*
When we speak of bunks, it's lower and upper,
But when we talk dentures, it's upper and lower,
And a hairdryer? Well, we just call it a *blower*!
Could it be that y'all are just a little bit slower?

Why is it inevitably <u>*out*</u> west, and <u>*back*</u> east?
And the opposite of <u>*famine*</u> is always <u>*feast*</u>?

West is to the left and the east is to the right,
The country's bucolic and the urban is blight?
Do you guys even know day from night?

You say _we won you_, and I say _we beat you_,
Now that you've won me, what will you do?
Caption me and put me in your trophy case?
Now that's not a win! That's a social disgrace!
Stay with me child…or get out of the race!

Now, this little narrative must come to an end,
I'm fine with _break_ if you're good with _bend!_
Because I didn't write all this stuff on a whim.
If you don't like my title, I'll call it _Us and Them!_
Then,
You guys will just have to sink or swim!
By (Who else?) Don Claybrook, Sr. AKA, Billy Bob!
March 5, 2021

What is it that you ponder, mostly? Get in touch with why _this_ and not _that_. Before you go on to the next chapter, ponder _this!_ It could tell you more about who you are, and the life you've lived, than anything else you could ever do. If you are much at all like I am, then you will be disappointed with some…and pleased with others. At that time you can leave the _this_ behind, and get on with the _that!_

Memories of West Texas
Acrylic by Don Claybrook, Sr.

Chapter 9
Poems about,

MEMORIES

Big Things, Little Things!

I'm thankful for the little things,
Like cinnamon skies and eagles' wings,
Like sorrow's tears that finally dry,
And lyrics that make a grown man cry.

I'm thankful for the big things too,
Like, *"Hi dad,"* and *"I love you."*
Like a natural smile on a newborn's face
And His incredible, Amazing Grace!
Date unknown

Camelot Again!

The grand days of Camelot,
Too soon were gone and now were not,
Nor soon forgot.
A new day's here,
Out damn spot!
Stand and cheer?

Does Time Wait?

Born in the great Lone Star State,
Couldn't wait to get out the gate.
So was it fate,
When it went wrong?
Time didn't wait,
For my song.
May 14, 2014

Highway 99!

Needles and Barstow,
Hell's hungry, haunting acres,
Only to be endured
For that ribbon of promise,
Called Highway 99!

Bakersfield, Turlock…
Other sun-blanched Meccas
Beckoning parched travelers
From Texas and sundry,
Barely remembered lands.

Oh, the time forgotten trails
We traced in search of Eden!
We pushed up our sleeves
And lingered awhile,
Our highway had
Taken us home.

We grew in numbers
And memories too…
(Mostly all golden),
And full of hope)…
On this road called
Ninety and Nine.

We waited…and,
we remembered.
But Time did neither.
In Sacramento
We wrote a history book.
Miners without a stake.
We pitched our tent
To stay awhile,

And live for another day.

To sing and cry
And recall again…
Of boys and girls
And highways,
Those days on 99.

Now…that highway
Is little more than a vestige.
Out of place, out of time,
And way out of the way.
But it showed us *"The Way."*

And not only took us *where* we are,
But made us *who* we are.

We grow old, but if we're fortunate,
We'll live a very long time.
But our highway will stay
Forever
99!
<u>Sometime in the early 1990's</u>

<u>Halcyon Days!</u>

Halcyon days and high schools,
The girls were hip and the guys fools.
But all kept there cools.
Now lost forever!
Time does have rules.
<u>They sever!</u>

Joey and Django!
(In three-letter words)

The era was bad and had nil nor naw,
She ran out her pup, and his wee bit paw,
'Til the kid who saw the *zig-zag* day sad,
Was the pup, and the kid, and her sad old Dad.

Who did dig the sun glo; for the fun was lux and gay,
But now hid his cry, and him did the bad guy pay.
Dad, all for the bit; ran the Alk (add the) eye!
Who had him *(sad to say),* 'til the big *"bye and the bye."*

The dog was Dja, *(and add)* ngo); and was her pet,
The pup did set his wag; and Dad had one eye wet.
And the pup let Dad pet him. Now, Dad was the boy!
The man did dig the dog; and his kid had her new toy.

Dad's gal saw the day, DJ's era did end; now she <u>did</u> cry.
For its act did not fit the bit; nor did her eye ere dry.
Her pup was now her big boy; and the dog was her sum,
He's now way out yon; and she, *"bye and bye"* did hum.

But she got out now, for she had fun; and, the all new gig,
Was her new pup?…all joy; was li'l, and not big.

The pup was Joe? Too li'l joy; Now add wye and hit the hay,
The all new duo, the kid and her dog, the new *pay-day!*

Joe is now the joy, the tit and the tat, and, her *"bad boy,"*
"The Man?" All the day has joy; Joe not nee, but coy.
The sun, the kid and the pup, all the way, but way too few.
Lay out the run for the day; and, bid the *"ev'r,"* sad ado.

Now the end, the old *pro-quo*, and all the eye's I did not dot,
Nor did the tee get hit. I've got the bit; and, salt got Mrs. Lot.
You? The mid-kid, Dad's own ACK, I've bid the old *"Now"* ado.
And bid you and Joey farewell for the day,
And thank Him, for these precious few.
<u>December 13, 2017</u>

<u>Lost Forever!</u>

Some years are lost forever,
Which we simply have to sever.
They were never,
Meant to stay.
Just an endeavor.
<u>Gone astray.</u>
<u>*2018*</u>

<u>My week!</u>

It was Sunday and the world was young,
And the rest was yet to be.
But only from the end of time,
Can honest prophets see.

They looked ahead, they looked behind,
And so far as they could tell,
The Sabbath jerked him from the cradle,
Through the reign of Hitler's Hell.

But Monday came with shouts of joy.
The darkest days were spent,
A time to reflect on yesterday,
Innocence about to be rent.

And as the sun raced through the ski,
And while the river ran,
He crossed the bridge of time and tense,
And slowly became a man.

Now Tuesday didn't give a damn
About the rest of the week.
For sight is lost and time stands still
When a man is at his peak.

So tie that knot as quick as you can,
With time you've called a truce.
Tuesday's your day for eternity,
Even as the knot works loose.

Yes, Wednesday came and brought an end,
To a week well on the run.
Turn out the lights, the fun is gone,
On a party just begun.

Wednesday was sad, it looked both ways,
A time to reflect...a pause,
Becoming aware in the midst of time,
That the week is governed by laws.

Thursday was vast nothingness,
A day to simply endure.
The past is but a memory,
The future has lost its lure.

The day dragged on for a long, long time.
It didn't really try.
The clouds of midday brought such pain,
But the evening refused to cry.

Now Friday was a bolt from the blue.
It came with a crisp, clear Call.
For those who only listen in springtime,
Are destined to hear in the fall.

Why, on Friday, when the week is waning,
When it seems one can do no wrong,
Is it time to slowly wind the week down,
And sing again, *"September's Song?"*

But, it really is a long, long time,
From May to December,
And Saturday…a day to cherish,
And a moment to remember.

The end of the week? Or, a brand-new day?
To loose one's soul and fly,
To a land of future memories,
And hopes up to the sky.

Now the Prophet is silent and his song is sung.
But his words ring loud and true.
We'll turn this day into a million,
And share these precious few.
Circa 1996

Pondering!

Why does my life, so short,
Reach for infinite time?
And why does my search yield shadows,
That mingle with thoughts sublime?
I find this inquiry appealing,
These questions that you pose.
Evoking in me a yearning,

For answers that nobody knows.
And so I ponder.

I ponder with even more questions,
For life is full of them.
But I rest in great assurance
That I rest best in Him.

But remember, my search yields shadows,
Not knowing from whence they stem.
Do you think that perhaps this darkness
Is the other side of Him?
And yet, I ponder.

Time is precious and time is short,
And time waits for no one, they say.
But as my time unfolds,
I yearn for one more day.

Yet what is time and what is light,
As we journey on this earth?
A thousand years of darkness,
Dispelled by one rebirth!
And still, I ponder.

I've heard it also said,
That at the break of day
When walking toward the light
The shadows fall away.

My thought now comes full circle,
I've missed it by a mile!
I need both light and shadow,
The shadow of your smile.

And here's what I've found.

Without the light there is no shadow,
No reach for infinite time.
Without our life together,
There is no other sublime.

For our love takes flight in timelessness
Making one our hearts, our souls,
Lost in love's sweet memory,
Fulfilling all our goals.
And ending all our pondering.

The answer is in the question
The student the teacher too.
We asked, we sought, we found,
And gave the Devil his due
Circa 1996-1999

Rain from Heaven!

A trip down memory lane,
Is seldom ever taken in vain.
However,
When we take a walk,
In heaven's rain.
Folks will think,
We've gone insane!
May 4, 2018

Remembering that Irish Spring!

My Dear Lady friend takes good care of me.
Mostly…I get good advice from Martha Lee,
Giving me her word, on everything I'll need,
Else…my life would go completely to seed!
A friend in need is a friend indeed,

Or quite possibly,
A San Angelo Stampede!
I learned that all Texans' voices are not pure,
Way back when she tried giving me the cure,
For hiccups that were just driving me insane.
A Texas lady cannot sing, <u>*The Rain in Spain*</u>!
The diction's a strain!
And the erstwhile best was a blessing in my life,
But you would have thought she was my wife,
When my feet began cramping so bad at night.
That I succumbed without even a decent fight!
That's just not right!
This *so-called* hiccup cure had got me thinking,
That Martha Lee had probably been drinking.
Since she never really got around to the point,
But did bring up <u>*Irish Spring*</u> for my ankle joint.
She was about to anoint!
"Put a bar of <u>Irish Spring</u> under the fitted sheet!"
(So now this is where science and voodoo meet).
"See if that soap won't cure your cramping ills."
I thought anything would be better than pills!
Like I need more thrills!
So, just four nights ago I thought I'd give it a try,
Feet hurting so badly could make a grown man cry!
I put two bars of <u>*Irish Spring*</u> under my fitted sheet,
Hoping the *thread-count* would let it get at my feet.
Well…that was indiscrete!
Since it didn't help, I guess I thought I'd been had!
Like when Mom took the car keys away from Dad!
See, Martha Lee never told me to unwrap the soap,
Guess she never thought I was that much of a dope!
I lost all hope!
To avoid a San Angelo Stampede,
I'd even try weed!
So next, I took the soap out of the nice green wrapper.

While not feeling quite so dumb…even a bit dapper!
But then this time I put the soap <u>above</u> the fitted sheet,
Just as close as I could get it next to my hurting feet!
This was it! *Trick-or-Treat!*
Well, wouldn't you know it, it worked like a charm!
But did you likewise know it would shoot up my arm?
That's what I'd call Sciatica going, not north, but south,
Leaving this old Texas cowboy…..down in the mouth!
Dry as a West Texas drouth!
So last night, I *duct-taped* a bar of soap to each foot,
T'was the strategic place, I thought, the soap to put.
Well wouldn't you know it, it worked out just right,
Until I had to get up and *"go"* in the dead of night!
Out of sight!
Well, you guessed it! I slipped and broke my dang hip,
Hush, Martha Lee, I don't want any *cotton-picking* lip!
From here on out, I think I'll just do my own doctoring,
And you stick to Tarleton State doing their proctoring!
No more inter-loctoring!
You might not be the wind beneath my wing,
But I'll remember forever that 2020 Spring,
When fate conspired with love so replete,
And you became the soap beneath my feet!
And that…is, oh so sweet!
Oh!
BTW, when can we meet?
<u>May 17, 2020, Revised February 15, 2022</u>

<u>Summertime Memories!</u>

I need no calendar to remind me that summer is almost gone.
There's a feeling in the air.
The change is almost imperceptible; yet, there is a difference.
Some of this summer's days will long be remembered.
They stand clear.

But most of them have already sifted through the sieve,
Of a fast-fading memory.
I also remember summer days from other times…
Days that should have long ago been forgotten.
They too stand clear.
Now as the season shifts ever so slightly,
My mind does the same,
Shifting from memories past to memories of the future.
They are not so clear.
But I'm content even as a new season unfolds,
Remembering that He has already been there.
And in that memory, I find sweet peace.
8/21/03

The Endless Struggle!

Civil rights are human rights,
And for them all mankind unites.
Fury always fights,
Sins to atone!
And recall slights,
Left alone.
2018

The 440 Yard Dash!

Yes, *"Stan the Man"* had a plan,
Refused to be an *"also ran!"*
Had his own brand.
He was a star!
And,
I was a fan,
From not so far.

Memories of Dad
Acrylic by Don Claybrook, Sr. in memory of my dad…and his Zinnias.

Zinnias!

Zinnias, Dad's favorite flowers,
Grew in gardens and on bowers.
Spent many hours,
And took great pride,
Had God's powers,
On his side.
May 27, 2019

Memories worth keeping are generally bathed in music. Music has an uncanny ability to make us remember time and place. If you want to have wonderful memories when you start nearing the "Golden Years," you'd be well advised to start now. Good music can surely make you yearn for the good old days; and, indeed can and do often make you mellow and nostalgic, and feeling somewhat depressed, and/or lonely. Which only proves my point. Music has a lasting effect on one's life. Make good music while you can!

The Claybrook Five!
Left to right: Don Jr., Landa Patrice, Autumn Claire, Liberty Jackson (Jack) and Don Sr.
Autumn Clairs wedding in Downtown Dallas, 2000!
Photo Credit Charlie Claybrook

CHAPTER 10
Poems about/for,

MY CHILDREN AND ME!

And When I Dream!

Jack, you mean the world to me,
And will…throughout eternity.
Love meant to be,
Forever new!
Who holds the key?
Me, Him, and You!
One plus two!
**Written on October 2, for the occasion of
your 25th Birthday, October 25, 2021**

Butterfly Days on Strawberry Point!

Butterfly days on Strawberry Point,
Flaxen hair in golden streams.
Your magic hill you did anoint,
And dream your butterfly dreams.

Those were your days to be alive,
To share your childhood joys,
Somewhere at the end of Seminary Drive,
Too busy living to think of boys.

Your nights were bathed with starlight,
From *The City by the Bay.*
The dark was tinged with twinkling twilight,
But your dreams, you dreamt by day.

Your magic kingdom had buildings and hills,
Sprinkled with bridges and valleys and knolls.
Mom worked all day to pay the bills,
While Dad *"did"* the Dead Sea Scrolls.

Your friends were Max, Britney and Lisa.
Your skies were mostly blue.

You explored a little bit of heaven, sans a visa,
And most of your dreams came true.

But, *"Butterfly Days"* on Strawberry Point,
Came to an end that fateful summer,
And somehow our dreams got all out of joint,
And again a preacher became a plumber.

So Autumn Claire, I loved you then,
With our hopes all full of tomorrow.
But to dream the dream, *"What might have been?"*
Is laden with too much sorrow.
Now those *"Butterfly Days"* are gone forever;
And I suppose, the preacher is too.
But neither time nor tide can sever,
This plumber's love for you.

So, be it just a day; or, a million light-years,
I'll choose not the end but the start.
And, we'll share our love with joy-filled tears,
Perhaps only in my dreams,
But always in my heart.
1987-1990 and revised on Nov. 26, 2017.
For my daughter, Autumn Claire (Claybrook) Kriofske.

Butterfly Free
(A birthday poem for my Sweet Liberty "Jack!")

Today is your birthday, Jack, it's number eleven,
For me it's been eleven years of heaven.
We danced on the night that you were born,
And marked the beginning of a brand-new morn.

I fell in love with you, some four months before your birth,
And now my love would move heaven and earth,

To watch a beautiful young child becoming all she can be,
While being joyful, delightful, and so *butterfly-free*.

So let's grab the years, and months and days,
To say, *"I love you,"* in a million ways.
And sing of rainbows and pots of gold,
The sweetest story ever told.
Happy Birthday, Child of my Dreams,
<u>On the occasion of your 11th Birthday.</u>
<u>Oct. 25, 2007.</u>

Donald Adrian Claybrook, Jr.
<u>My son, at home in Santa Rosa California, 2018</u>
Photo Credit: Becky Claybrook, my *daughter-in-law!*

Don Jr.

We knew he was pretty bright when he was about six,
Took a smidgen more to babysit him than *Pick-Up-Stix!*
Had an adult sense of humor, knew *double entendre.*
Liked computers! Didn't think much of doing laundry!
From the looks of his room!
One day he went with me to Strawberry Shopping Center.
His outer expressions and things, seldom matched his inner.
Saw an aisle full of diapers, Pampers and stuff that smells,
And with the slightest smile he said *"Look Dad. Pie shells!"*
Because he knew that I knew!
He knew the well-known story…I hated changing diapers!
I'd rather milk a snake, or be shot at by terrorist snipers!
Which of course led to my disdain for yuck! Pumpkin pies!
And people telling me how good it was, and all those lies!
If they only knew, but…they hadn't a clue.

So, Strawberry Point Elementary School tested him one day,
And he blew the top out of their third grade test in every way.
"May we take Donny to Palo Alto for Stanford-Binet testing?"
"Yes! It's OK with us," we said, hoping his brain wasn't resting!
On the day they were suggesting for the testing.

We came to learn that our son had a very rare intelligence indeed!
He's mom and I took some comfort in knowing we sewed the seed!
But we learned after many fits and more than a modicum of starts,
That our son was rare indeed! And greater than the sum of the parts!
At the risk of casting darts…at our son's *"smarts."*

Straight from high school he was sent to Navy Nuclear School.
Where, even on their worst day, they seldom if ever, invited a fool.
On the night of graduation, he and most of his class celebrated,
If you call getting drunk festive! Actually they miscalculated!
And the Navy ceased providing their gravy! Terminated!

But, after marrying his Probation Officer, first name Becky,
He got into computer stuff and became a world-class techie!
In time they had a beautiful daughter, Named her Abigail!
Now there's no need for them to have that *Wishing Well!*
Life is swell, and oh so good!
When one does, what one should!
<u>Oct. 24, 2021</u>

<u>Don Jr. Turns 53!</u>

He came into my life in the year, *Nineteen Sixty-Nine!*
His sister, Claire, preceded him by about 16-months.
They were quite a pair, these two offspring of mine,
Always up to non-noxious mischief, or pulling stunts.
Then,
Life took Donny from Stockton CA to *Old Big-D.*
Mill Valley, Louisville, and then on to Beaumont!
Back to Indiana, then on an unknown moving spree!
Then back to the Golden State, drinking of that font!
Now,
While Dad was at Golden Gate on a three-year stay.
Donny went through third, and then on to Kentucky.
Where he graduated from Jeff High along the way,
And then serendipity struck, and Don Jr. got lucky!
How so?
He met a lady named Becky! And the rest is history!
But Don Jr. had to wait, Miss Becky was quite taken.
No! Not with Donny! He wasn't part of the mystery!
She was already married. Talk about being shaken!!!
Nevertheless,
As fate would have it, God works in mysterious ways,
His wonders to perform! His grace is still amazing!
Donny and Becky would remember all of their days.
Both stormy days and days that were lazily dazing.
But,
They finally got together and our Lord sent a Song!

Abigail Ivie was born, and the skyrockets went off.
This sweet gift from our Lord could do no wrong,
At a phone booth in Paris, I was higher than a loft!
Because I knew!
What a man never knows! The joy a daughter can bring,
Until one appears in his life, changing his orientation,
From the moment he does, *"Abigail"* has a golden ring,
Which can magically make Dad, an overnight sensation!
So this!
Donny, I love you, Son! More than I can say in verse,
You mean so much to me! I'm glad my only son is you!
Your mom could not have done better! I deserve worse.
But between you and your Sis, and my other Two too,
And grace from beyond the blue,
I'm the richest man I know…for an Old So and So!
Written for my Son on the occasion of his 53rd Birthday! February 2, 2022

Don Sr.
Photo credit: Willie Ann Comte,
My maternal grandmother.

Don Jr.
Photo credit: Shirley Claybrook,
Donny's Mom.

From a Jack to a King!

For very much of my life I wandered, and logged a'many a'mile,
Never knowing where I would land… just living life with a smile.
While roaming from one place to another, a hunger haunted me,
Building a life with reckless abandon…Now that would set me free!

I built my dreams on *stardust,* which would ultimately be my loss,
While wagering my life so foolishly on *"one game of pitch and toss."*
I sought my life's meaning in education, with diplomas and degrees,
While hardly ever discerning, they were like the forest and the trees.

There are so many diplomas I've taken, so many degrees I've earned,
Hard to tell the forest from the trees, I've forgotten all I ever learned.
Time never stands still, though we're not mindful of that when young.
Like Don Quixote fighting windmills, dancing with the one we brung.

But why is being so footloose and so quixotic, thought to be so very wrong,
When all one really wants from life is to love; and, to sing *September's Song*?
I honestly and fully fell in love with her, many months before she was born.
And as I reflect back on those halcyon days, they make me feel very forlorn.

For what about life is worth living, when it all fades into the setting sun?
When God sends a beautiful baby, a daughter, bringing so much joy and fun.
And so I ponder and remember, Liberty Jack, the choices you and I made,
Stacking firewood and reading Bible stories and all the games we played.

Do I miss and regret the loss of all those wonderful days and nursery rhymes?
What do you think Liberty? Do <u>you</u> miss them too? <u>Those were the best of times</u>!
Days and memories I can never have again, because of the choices we chose,
Lost to me for eternity, they are forever gone, the moments in time we froze.

But as surely as God works His wonders, and you hit that *<u>twenty-first year,</u>*
Know that I celebrate <u>what we had</u>…what remains, I celebrate with a tear.
For if I drew a line in the sand, relentlessly pointing to a Perfect Spring,
I would ever remember that October, when I went *From a Jack to a King!*

So, on this 25ᵗʰ day of October, 2017, I wish you a Happy 21ˢᵗ birthday, my, Sweet Jack,
And wish for you this gift this day…the greatest gift of all,
I WISH YOU LOVE!
Written and given with love on the occasion of your 21ˢᵗ birthday, October 25, 2017, your dad and your friend.

Landa Patrice
The wedding of my first Daughter who lives in Corpus Christi Texas
With my grandson, Jimmy John. Photo: T.L. Johns

Landa Patrice!

Born eight days after December,
On a cold night in Waco, I well remember!

I didn't cry Hurrah! More like, *"Timber!"*
I had to work!
No heat! Not even an ember!
And my boss was a jerk….
That January in December,
As best I remember.
She's neither my sister nor my niece,
She's my *first-born* child, Landa Patrice!
I wish her joy, and a 62nd year,
That is merry and mild and filled with cheer!
Happy 61st birthday, Baby Girl! I love you, Dad,
January 8, 2020, composed 01/03/2020

Landa Patrice
Photo by T.L. Johns

Liberty Jackson Claybrook!
(A Tribute)

I've spent the last 21 years saying and writing *"good words"* about Liberty Jackson Claybrook. I count it a wonderful opportunity to do so on this most auspicious occasion, her graduation from Chico State University. (I find it almost impossible to believe I just typed that last line). Where have those 22 years gone? Yes, I did say 22 years. She won't be 22 until October 25; but, that was not a misstatement nor a typo. I fell in love with this young lady when she was still basking securely within the safe haven of her mother's womb. By the time she saw the light of day, this dad was totally smitten…and still am today.

When she finished high school at Mendocino High and then headed off to Chico to put in her time there, I was sad…and yes, quite lonely. I sat down and penned a poem for her 21st birthday that includes these lines:

For if I drew a line in the sand, relentlessly pointing to a Perfect Spring,
I would ever remember that Friday, when I went from a Jack to a King!

Yes, she entered this world in October; but, that fall day became the best and most beautiful spring day the good Lord ever made. God was so very good to me when He sent this unspeakable joy from heaven. Her mom and I called her *"Jack"* from the very beginning. That tiny baby girl, that Jack, made me a king on that October night in 1996. I suppose you had likely already guessed that by now.

Now, Jack's graduation approaches and I am so very proud of her. She is that *"once in a million"* person who comes along all too seldom…one of whom I can honestly say, *"Liberty Jackson Claybrook is greater than the sum of the parts."* I'm sure her mom would also agree with that assessment.

I believe she will hold a special place in her heart for Chico State. I know she will hold *Gamma Phi Beta* dear to her heart always.

A big *"THANK YOU"* to her sorority sisters; and, blessings to those educators who brought her safely through it all. And to my baby girl I say once again:

Time never stands still, though we're not mindful of that when young.
Like Don Quixote fighting windmills, just dance with the one you brung.
Jack, just keep on going with the Lord. He's brought you safe thus far.
Nor will He ever forsake you. He's your *Bright and Morning Star!*

Dad, on the occasion of your graduation from Chico State, May 18, 2018

My Special Winkle!

I knew a Winkle, once upon a time.
This little Winkle was a friend of mine.
She was always with me, never wandered far.

She was neither a shadow, nor a far-away star.

She would winkle her eyes and winkle her nose,
And grace my life with pretty rainbows.
The sun would shine wherever she went.
My Winkle was surely heaven sent!

This Winkle would cry and giggle and sing,
And make my heart go *"Ping! Ping! Ping!"*
My Winkle would sparkle like diamonds and dew,
And stormy skies would turn sky-blue.

This Winkle would shine, this Winkle would beam,
My Winkle brought me a *"Stardust-Dream."*
My Winkle was a song, a natural high.
My Winkle was a sweet lullaby.

My Special Winkle makes work feel like play,
And makes me want to laugh every day.
And sends me off to *Never, Never,*
And make me want to live forever.

The days would come and the years would go,
And like a sapling, my Winkle would grow.
Who is this Winkle that fills my days?
And lights my nights in a thousand ways?

Her name is Liberty. We call her Jack,
From the distaff side of the railroad track.
That means she's a girl…and not a boy.
Today she's three + three, my life, my joy!

She's six years old and pretty as a kitten.
She's my dream come true. I'm Winkle smitten!
Oct. 25, 2002 on the occasion of Jack's sixth birthday.

Liberty Jackson (Jack) Claybrook
My last daughter who turned 25 on October 25, 2021
Photo Credit, Rainbow School, Mendocino California, 2000.

Summertime Reflections!

Where in the world does springtime go,
When the sun decides to give us a show,
When summer demands its place in time,

And brightly comes out, with a heavenly chime?

Summer always infringes, on springtime's song,
But the seasons fade, they don't last too long.
And they bring to an end the *"Perfect Season."*
And for why? We don't know the reason.

But as for the longevity of summer, we can only smile,
And be thankful for the memories, our hearts will file,
In the memory bank of our minds, captured every day.
As the amber hues of autumn quickly find their way.

Yes, the seasons fade away, so much like a mist,
And leave this earth knowing, it's truly been kissed.
Away with all our *"Whys,"* and our *"Wherefores,"*
Summer too will pass, in rhythm with all our folklores.

And when this summer's gone, after not so very long,
Might we two just once again, sing September's Song?
For the bright colors of autumn, are as surely to follow,
As Capistrano beckons, to the very last swallow.

And then we will remember, that Nature has its rules,
Just as surely as remembering, that the world has its fools.
That the seasons will come, and with clockwork will flow,
Whence they come, whither they go…will we ever really know?

So, on this beautiful summer night, let's sing our song of life,
And celebrate once again, putting aside all rancor and strife.
And know in our hearts, that heaven's choir will sing,
When all God's children simply and completely,
Let love rule supreme.
By Don Claybrook Sr. and Liberty *"Jack"* Claybrook, via email,
<u>From Monday Evening, July 3, to Friday, July 7, 2017</u>

The Cookie Monster Caper!

I spent quality time with my baby girl today,
Time I thought was gone forever.
Time which I'd lost somewhere along the way.
Time I'd likely not redeem…for-never.
So, no, I'm not saying I drove to Chico,
Nor was she in Fort Bragg.
No, our get-together was courtesy of a sly *peek-O*.
Thanks to iPhone and a trick right out of the bag.

With nothing better to do, I decided to eat an oatmeal cookie.
Now I'm no expert cameraman. In fact, I'm nothing but a rookie.
But before I did, I grabbed my iPhone and took a photo.
But I'll swear that cookie looked somewhat like *Quasimodo*.

So, she and I traded texts two ways, post and back.
And, I took a bite from another, right out of the sack
I had that girl thinking that cookie was lunar,
Put her picture in gap and called it *Gap-Girl-in-Mooner*.

She just called it simply, *The Oatmeal Cookie Caper*.
I'll admit it was weird, but it sounded good on paper.
That's when I proclaimed, *"I'm the Cookie Moonster!"*
But truth be known, I was just being a *Loony Toonster!*

And so, I'll admit it. I'll take time with my precious Jack any old way it will fit.
Even if I have to take a picture of an oatmeal cookie, making up a story I've writ.
Now you know all that I do. But wait, every good tale always adds a P.S. at the bottom.
Mine is a half-moon oatmeal cookie. Why? Well perhaps, just because I've got 'em.
April 27, 2018

Liberty Jackson (Jack) in a Cookie!
Photo credit: Don Claybrook, Sr.

Three and One!

I had three daughters; one son,
In my heart ere time had begun.
More said than done,
But always knowing,
Our children are a garden,
So,
Keep on hoeing!

Don Jr., Landa Patrice, Autumn Claire,
Liberty Jackson (Jack) and Don Sr…
Elk California!
Photo Credit: Charlie Claybrook

To My Son!
(Don Claybrook, Jr.)

Well now I've been neglecting,
But also doing a bit of reflecting,
And detecting!
And here's what's true:
When it comes to expecting,

Had I but one son,
And not a few,
I'd always want,
That one,
To be you!
<u>Oct. 24, 2021</u>

Autumn Claire on Strawberry Point!
Don Claybrook, Sr. Photo Credit: Don Claybrook, Sr.

Yellow Roses for a Mellow Lady!
(For my precious daughter Autumn Claire)

You've reached that golden milestone, Autumn Claire,
My lovely daughter with the beautiful flaxen hair.
If beauty is the way you roll, then you are most nifty.
As pretty as a burnished sunset, as you turn…Yes, 50!

I recall a memory of somewhere, at the end of that first year,
The picture of a baby girl, holding a telephone to her ear.
Your face shone with joy and happiness, there was no guile,
Innocence captured in a studio window, forever…for a while.

She and her baby brother Donny, quite the dynamic two,
Would challenge that innocence many times…not a few.
They cut quite a caper, oftentimes just to dance and shout,
Only perceptively stopping, when dad bellowed, _"Cut it out!"_
The years hastened by, hardly leaving her time to ponder,
The mysteries of life, much less beyond the great yonder.
She was busy with classes, degrees, marriage and such,
Not always aware, that not enough, is often, too much.

My golden-haired-beauty, <u>carried</u> a heavy burden of anguish and strife,
For she knew, down deep in her soul, that she wanted <u>to carry</u> new life.
So, my precious lady, you'll never know, how much your hurt shed new light.
I was blind, but your love for the world's _"Django's,"_ gave me back my sight.

On the occasion of your 50th birthday, when all is said…but hardly done,
I hope and pray your _fifty-first_ year, will be by far, your very best one.
And most of all, I wish you that gift, that can only come from above,
With all my heart, with all my soul, with all my best wishes,
I wish you love*
*(Because "Love never fails." I Corinthians 13:8a)
Written in early August and given on the occasion of your 50th birthday, September 26, 2017
<u>On August 26, 2017</u>

Autumn Claire in The Kitchen!
Photo Credit: Autumn Claire, Selfie.

One can readily see, as we come to the end of this category, family is important to me! That of which poets write, tells you more about the poet than anyone else…

"White Water in the Mist!"
Watercolor by my daughter, Liberty Jackson "Jack" Claybrook-Reyes

Chapter 11
Poems about

LOVE'S LOST AND FOUND

A Bell With No Clapper!

Don't you recall when our love was fresh and new?
When days and nights were filled with utmost joy?
We had our special dreams and shared quite a few,
Reflecting on life together, like kids with a new toy.
Time stood still!
We happily talked half those nights and days away,
And we laughed like two kids on a *merry-go-round*.
You were a memo written on my heart, *"Someday!"*
Could it really be that at last I was heaven bound!
Was it His will?
The days passed and the months began to blend,
And it looked like we were about to seal the deal.
Stars showed the way like they had for wise men,
And God was tending to us, His *Lilies of the Field*.
On Cypress Ridge Hill and in *"The Ville!"*
Everything was perfect except for that <u>ONE</u> thing,
We both knew what it was...and what it was doing.
Because a bell without a clapper refuses to ring.
And my memory knew that a storm was brewing.
Ink without a quill!
The question's neither who to blame, nor not to blame,
Nor is there a problem of incompatibility either.
No, the fly in the ointment has a different name,
Our choice remained between Never and Neither!
And a political standstill!
Will we become one, or remain just good friends,
And just go on with our lives totally unchanged?
Or will we finally see the evil and make amends?
The future depends on our lives being rearranged.
For,
Without a clapper, the bell simply will not ring!
And without time, life would just stands still.
But now the lonely singer has come to sing,
Without further ado, it's time to pay the bill!

It was so easy to fall in love with you, Martha Lee,
And yet, strangely, we two have never met.
But if I live to be one-hundred and three,
Your sweet loving face, I'll never forget.
But, a house divided cannot stand!
<u>When built on sinking sand.</u>

<u>A Sonnet for Charlie!</u>

My life was adrift in an angry sea,
When a sudden twist of fate, brought her to me,
Gone was the longing, as dark and dank as sin.
No longer dreaming, what might have been.

Now the skies are blue, not a cloud in sight,
The days spent together, absolute delight,
And every night is sunshine and joy.
I'm younger by a mile, a *man-child* boy.

Then my world turned upside down, inside out,
I wonder, *"What was she thinking about,"*
When she took my life, Liberty, my joy.
Treating my heart like a *wind-up* toy?

On some distant summer day, I'll dream again,
Of *graced-love* and Charlie;
And what might have been.
<u>May 2, 2015</u>

<u>Beauty is Fragile!</u>

Beauty is best when in love,
When it thrives on light from above's,
Innocent dove.
When bad things count,

Push comes to shove,
And,
Discords mount,
As lost as love.
May 2, 2018

Because I Remember!

I took black and whites,
When she and I played in the rain,
Because I wanted to remember.
I carved her name on a plank of wood,
On a rail in the overlook by the beach,
Because I didn't want to forget.
I let her go because I couldn't keep her,
But because I couldn't forget her,
I couldn't let her go.
Because I Remember

Four-Letter Word Poem!

Alas! *Morn-tide*, soon here with very fine rain,
Also hope runs high, dark sky's gone away,
Wish none less than this mist, sans some pain.
Hour upon hour…same evil song must play.

Ever this cold! Same lame word, same dull tune,
Then, away with what ails, this gray, blue tale,
Best when four feet meet upon *sand-grit* dune.
Hope will come anew, when this dark goes pale.
They were here, live…each soul with God's good love.
Pure evil. Also some came back, like Noah's *twig-dove*.
Abel, Cain, Marx, Heil! Salk, King, Ruth, also Lot's wife,
Love, hate, each soul must wait; then, God dots each life,

…

He connects those dots with love; and, with a very straight line,
I'm one of those dots. I answered his invitation to *come and dine*.
And I remember with joy when He said, *"Whosoever will may come."*
Trying to say all that in a *four-letter-word* poem, is just plain dumb.
Just as then, now, I give up. And that has made all the difference.
<u>Completed on January 25, 2018</u>

<u>Friday!</u>

'T'was a day I can't ignore,
That Friday she slipped out my door.
I walk the floor,
From dusk to dawn,
But forevermore,
She'll be gone.
<u>May 24, 2019</u>

<u>Guile or Innocence?</u>

Guile has its proponents too,
Giving each event unjust due.
Out of the blue
Comes common sense.
A brighter hue,
<u>Innocence.</u>

<u>Hello Darling!</u>

I want you to meet a new friend of mine,
From dear old Texas, on the railroad line.
I haven't really known her for very long,
But she has my heart just singing a song.

Her hometown, and pretty face on Facebook,
Caused me to take a very careful second look.

So with trepidation, I introduced myself to her,
And every day since then has been a hazy blur.

The days passed by…and the nights they did too,
And our messages on Messenger just fairly flew.
We've talked about everything from soup to nuts,
And like old Dandy Don, even *"ifs"* and *"buts!"*

Now I'm a pretty good judge of weather and people,
For I can read them both like the sky does a steeple.
The lady is beautiful and just as nice as she can be,
She's a friend of mine…as anyone can see!

Now, I've been so lonely…my cupboard was bare,
And it remains to be seen if there's a *"there"* there!
But as *Father Time* passed from yesterday to now,
That question has been answered. And oh boy! How!

So now, let's give the answer as quickly as can be,
Was there a *there,* there? There was! For you see,
I don't know about you, maybe your cupboard's bare
But as for me…well…My Lord answers prayer!
Don Claybrook, 2021

Husbands and Wives!

Of all the sad facts of life.
Filled with much bitterness and strife,
Husband and wife!
Rowboats a'going
Cuts like a knife
Keep on rowing!

I'd Trade It All!

I'd trade all of my yesterdays,
And not regret any of the ways,
My old mind plays.
If I could be,
For all my days,
With Martha Lee!
Dec. 22, 2019

Lightening in a Bottle!

I've heard it said_, "He caught lightening in a bottle."_
The truth be told, I did. And I embraced it full throttle.
Yes, I experienced that incredible joy _once upon a time_,
And put a seal on it, to lock in that lightening sublime.

But, the cork would finally blow out like an ember glow.
I asked Him to put the lightening back; but, He said _"No."_
I didn't take that as a final answer. I refused to let it go,
Learning in the doing there was really no _quid-pro-quo._

My world was dark, my heart was broken, I wanted to go.
So I did, over the globe. From Reno to Chico and Santiago,
To Sacramento and Fresno and even Benbow and Encino.
I think you have it. I went anywhere the wind would blow.

My life met with disparity, much like Plato and Trevino;
Like the brothers DiMaggio, No, not Dom but Jolting Joe.
Or Dino, Gino and Marino. From Alaska to Old Mexico.
Kept on looking for that lost lightening and its after-glow.

I wore a turban and a sash, tried a crewcut and even an afro.
And made many new friends; but, I also met an unlikely foe.
A broken heart with memories that just would not let me go.
There is very little distance between…say…Wade and Roe.

My baby girl was not aborted; nor, did she ever really know,
For hurting would be my constant companion, a life of woe.
My new abiding place, much like an igloo is to an Eskimo.
Where the tears never dry; and, where *angels still fear to go.*

The *hurting place* is real and so are the memories that flow.
The magic of Santa Fe, enchantment, like hues in a rainbow.
And the magnificence that is Lake Louise, I will always know.
I'd sooner forget the Alamo than the Canadian Rocky's snow.

This I've learned in the year of our Lord, 2018 Anno Domino,
That I've every reason to cherish love and hope, friend and foe.
Every right to infer and ask, as I ponder my fate here below,
<u>This:</u>
Where did the lightening go? That caused me to fall in love,
So many years ago.
Magic lightening was long ago; but, the hurt seems to grow.
The days, and nights, and months and years go by quite slow,
And my search for it has come to a rather abrupt end; and, so,
If Love never fails, lightening from out of the blue will go,
<u>Bingo!</u>
And will fill my bottle again to overflow. Then I will know.
Love's sweet, warm afterglow!
<u>May 23, 2018</u>

<u>Look into My Eyes!</u>

What do you see when you look into my sad old eyes?
Will you please venture beyond my look of sorrows?
Perhaps glimpsing the *all-enchanting* look of surprise,
Now exposing my daydreams of beautiful tomorrows.

I've spent so much of my life just searching for you,
Without any vision or notion of who or what you are.
I knew if I were lucky, my dreams <u>*might*</u> come true,
Shunning my past, my present searching near and far.

When I gaze into your eyes and bury my soul there,
My heart swells to a state of rapture, about to burst,
And it beats almost more than reason can lay bare,
As I ponder a love that goes from *dead-last* to first.

Yes, I think it's true, I loved you before you were born,
Love made in heaven and reserved for <u>some</u> *"Someday,"*
A love that would endure hell's wrath and yet still adorn,
The shadow you cast, from here to *Kingdom-Come Day.*

Please reach out and take this rough old cowboy's hand,
And witness a dying man rise from the grave and thrive.
Your sweet smile will beam me to *Hope's Happy Land,*
Where a once dead lump of clay will again come alive.

But you will never know how much I hurt unless you look,
And see sweet lullabies are often little more than bitter lies.
Then that's when you will learn just what this moment took.
The melody of love will die, unless you gaze into my eyes,
And read *My Heart's Book!*
Please look!
June 29, 2019

Love in Bloom!

A conspiracy is neither cute,
Nor an intellectual pursuit.
It's best left mute!
But,
Alas and forsooth!
When love takes root,
Like gin and vermouth,
Two loves blend,
And cherish Truth!
June 1, 2021

Love Is a Three-Letter Word!

His Son, *"The Way"* had his say,
But for Him, we'd all die for our sin.
And was the one, who won the day.
And, won the war, for all men.

"The Way," God's one Son,
Did Buy off and tip the bar.
The two did sue and ban the dun;
The Duo, who, for the *"uns,"* are.

And we'd dip and sip and sup,
And our Lord, did not get lax,
Who did get for you the cup.
And win for all, the sum <u>and</u> tax.

He'd buy our map; run and sue,
And had not, but for his vow,
Did say *"aye"* for all the few,
And all woe and foe did bow.

The end was day-hue red.
And the sky was mid-aft tan.
He'd see the *"had not"* fed and led,
Now The Man and God, was but One,
And God, *"The Son Man!"*
December 13, 2017

Moonlight!

We've not met, but I can see,
Moonlight becomes you, Martha Lee!
Here then is the key,
After all that pain.

Our lives will be,
Love's sweet refrain.
Because love never fails!
April 3, 2020

My Baby Girl!

She said she'd stay for a spell,
Had my heart ringing like a bell.
But, truth to tell,
She left that day
And,
It hurt, like
Hell…is here to stay.
May 6, 2019

My Once Upon a Valentine: (The Original)!

I searched the whole world through, my heart was broken.
"What might have been," filled all my lonely days.
And when you said, *"I do,"* well, I said, *"I do too."*
I'd found my valentine, where dreams come true.

We left *bluebonnet-land;* where dreams are born,
And lingered in…old, New Mexico.
The Badlands were enchanted too, and all because of you,
The bad times were gone, my skies were always blue.

Out in the Golden State, we built our new life;
But things got hard, and all the gold was gone.
You were growing restless, while I was growing old.
"What might have been," the saddest story ever told.

I dream of our sweet vows, and my sweet valentine,
But all my dreams are stardust memories.

I'll sing September's song, the rest of my days,
And ponder a million times, her sweet, amazing ways,
My once upon a valentine.
Written and revised November 28, 2017

My Once Upon A Valentine! (Revised)
(A song)

Charlie girl, Charlie girl, you are my Valentine.
Charlie girl, Charlie girl, until the end of time.
Charlie girl, my Valentine, God gave you to me,
And then He made *"forever"* so we could have a time to be.

We had, to leave the land, where the blue, bonnets grow,
So we stopped… for a while…in old New Mexico.
The Badlands were enchanting, and Santa Fe too,
But Charlie girl, my Valentine, it was all because of you.

From Santa Fe, we drove out west, to the Golden State,
But the gold, was all gone, we were a few years too late.
The days flew by, Charlie girl, and I was getting old,
But like a blue north Texas wind, your love was growing cold.

You gave me, our Valentine, on a cool October night,
She and I danced, to *Stardust,* as I gently held her tight.
But now you've taken, sweet Liberty, away from me,
Leaving me, a broken man, with a *Stardust* memory.

Charlie girl, my sweetheart, you *were,* my Valentine!
Charlie girl, my cameo, our vows were so divine.
I promised you, Valentine, 'til death do us part,
But now, you say you want, a brand new start.

I'll love you, Valentine, as long as stars shall shine,
But from May, to December, is a long and lonely time.

And Charlie girl, *"forever,"* was way, too short,
So when the nights are lonely, I will hold you in my heart.

But Charlie girl, there's one thing, that to me is so sublime,
The precious memories of you, and our baby Valentine.
So, you'll always be, my sweet Charlie, *My Once Upon a Valentine.*
And sweet Liberty, you will also be, *My Once Upon a Valentine.*
(Upon Charlie's leaving me and taking Jack with her…circa 2010.)

Stop this Train!

Thought the whole world had my back,
And that I was on the right track.
Then I lost Jack,
My sweet refrain.
Clickity clack,
Stop this train!
May 13, 2019

Surprised by Love!

I suppose I will forever dream and wonder,
Becoming one, as lightning and thunder,
Of the gentle way she eased into my life.
The miracle! When she became my wife.

Sweetness was that magic she possessed,
Etched into my heart and deeply recessed,
Leaving its mark, which left many traces,
Never-ending love…in all the right places.

My honest impressions, when I ponder back,
Each night was starlit…in twinkling black,
Days always filled with Love's first sunrise.
And miracle moments, an absolute surprise!

We moved down close to the Pacific Ocean,
I was at peace, no rush, nor wasted motion,
Living out all our days, with incredible joy.
Man on a mission, with only love to deploy.

An enchanted land! Could anything be better?
Wondrous joy, neither time nor age could fetter,
Two lovers as one…with all things we'd cope.
Needing only our Lord, and His whispering hope.

Then a White Dove appeared, and blessed our soul,
A most precious baby girl, He gave for us to hold.
Kissing our lives with a divine promise…a birth!
Joy unspeakable, and priceless beyond all worth!

As is their custom, many days turned into years,
Making my life complete, with floods of joy's tears,
Our baby girl became a lovely lady, with not a care,
Bringing us Life and Liberty, a breath of fresh air!

Just when life was getting, as good as life can be,
Evil came into our lives, something I could not see.
My good world changed, it would never be the same.
Three Lives torn apart…I pondered…am I to blame?

Only God will ever know, what hell on earth can be,
So, as I reminisce, my thoughts are reminding me,
Love and life are gone, only my memories remain.
Yesterday's wine and paradise lost, what a sad refrain.

I loved you so much, like no one before has ever done,
Our love was made to endure. Its equal? There was none!
A Love for which I've moved heaven and earth…to reprise.

And, what will I remember? Losing my morning sun,
And…forever and always, love's <u>heartbreaking surprise!</u>
<u>July 18, 2017</u>

What I felt!

Do I really deserve this?
What have I done, what did I miss?
This deadly kiss,
Has left me cold.
A deep abyss,
Fills my soul.
May 27, 2019

When Love Dies!

It happened in a heartbeat,
The day that love died on our street.
I still repeat,
Years e'er I knew,
Life's but a cheat,
It's really true!
May 27, 2019

When Love Intrudes!

A heart that's been broken, cannot be repaired.
Since I am not immune, I will not be spared,
From bearing the burden of unspent years.
Living my life with nothing, but hope's fears.

Hope takes second place to fear. It simply waits,
Discerning my shattered dream that never abates.
Reflecting alone, I quietly ponder, night and day,
What went so very wrong? I cannot honestly say.

But, an unexpected miracle, caresses my consciousness,
The miracle of love, that gives me repose from my duress,
And rekindles a hope that Truth will surely prevail.
Knowing that fear will fade away, and love will never fail.

Some call it a miracle, when love rips history's veil,
What has been hidden, I believe, transcends the pale.
When again, for the first time, we see face to face.
Neither myth nor miracle, but His Amazing Grace.
April 27, 2015

When Ought…Should!

When you hear love's sweetest call,
Think not that you're too big to fall.
Don't stand too tall,
When things look good,
And when they stall
Then ought…should,
Become would!

When Push Comes to Shove!

Beauty is best when in love,
When it thrives on light from above,
Pure as a dove!
But,
When bad things count
Push comes to shove
Discords mount.

Yesterday's Snow!

It was a time to be filled with contentment and joy,
With the hopes of tomorrow coming early by a day,
A time for an old man once again to become a boy,
A heart beating with life and love, come what may.

Your answer was No! Not today, nor tomorrow. Never!
And a bit of irony thrown in to make the loss complete.

But nothing can save what naught but hate can sever.
Hope's victory that was destined to become its defeat.

The hurt goes on as I think of what might have been,
What all my tomorrows were, I thought, meant to be.
Now that you've spoken, terrible loss replaces a win,
I was so blind and such a foolish man, I could not see.

Wrap it all up in lots of old newspaper and trash it.
The end has come. Indeed, the end is all that I know.
I'll just go on with my life with the candle barely lit,
Little is left, gone like footprints in yesterday's snow.

<u>September 12, 2018</u>

By the end of this Chapter 11, I realize that I'm somewhat of an expert on this topic, Loves lost and loves found. That is to say, I've likely made all the mistakes one man can make with my 3 failed marriages. And, if practice makes perfect, I'm an expert in this field! Oh, to be clear, one marriage lasted 26 years and another 21, but, all ended with the other party filing for divorce. My first marriage was a total failure because one of us was trying to escape a home for very good reasons, while the other was trying to escape home, for little or no valid reason. I fit the latter category. The next two marriages were good and happy marriages for the most part…and I was surprised when they came to an end. Perhaps that was the biggest problem. That I was surprised is most likely an indication that I wasn't paying attention.

So, the bottom line is this, from this *"expert."* Thank God that you were fortunate enough to find the right one from the start. And possessed the acute discernment to see it and know it. You're a lucky man, and, or woman

Reflections on 2021!
**Photo Credit: The Point Cabrillo Lighthouse Association, Mendocino California,
Where I serve as a docent for Supervisor of Docents, Jen Lewis.**

CHAPTER 12
Tips For,

LIFE AND LOVE

A Reflection on 2021!

Dear Friend or Foe/Brother/Sister, or no!
The last day of the year is always a day of reflection for me. Lots of memories were made....and
some unmade! Thanking my Lord that He brought me through it all. Indeed, thanking him
that I've never been more healthy in ANY 10 year span of my life than I have been in the,
current 10 years! Mentally, physically, emotionally and spiritually (some might
question one or two of those) I cannot explain it, but I
accept it with a grateful heart. .May your 2022
be one to remember....With much
love/respect/chagrin, etc.
Don Claybrook, Sr.
P.S. Forgetting the past and pressing on to the mark of the high calling of God in Jesus Christ!
...

ABC's of Life!

Life is like a recipe with many unknown ingredients,
Met with both myriad evils and a loving expedience.
The unexamined life, they say, is not worth the living,
It's like the Dead Sea, always receiving, never giving.

Alphabetically speaking, might just give it a perspective,
Birth is only a beginning. Life lived makes us reflective.
Caring is a dimension of life....keeping one in the know,
Daring is ofttimes foolish but, we need to be in the show.

Easy living? No...but it's hardly ever wrong to daydream.
Friends are proverbial, they're just like peaches and cream.
Giving is the greatest example of love, there can be no doubt,
Hard, yes...but a life graced by love, is what it is all about.

Infinite: Everlasting, never ending, eternal time and place.
Justice is... what? Who can define it, can discern its face?
Kindness is related to Justice...lending it space and room.
Love...the root of Justice, and the Kindness that will bloom.

Money has its lovers too, a love leading to danger and death.
Nothingness is a philosophy…breathing its very last breath.
Oppression its goal; and, denying its Creator, its evil caress!
Pretending life is about nothing, not even their own duress.
Quality: a state of mind, the hallmark of life, the place to begin.
Real is its perfect description, authenticity its nearly perfect twin.
Stop, lay back, take time to enjoy, find a brand new way to roll.
Time never stands still…Take a little of it, just to rest your soul.

Unassuming is a strange word, but it has that certain something.
Veracity is the nature of truth, beguiling, and with an honest ring.
Wonder makes dreamers out of the worst of us; the world stops!
Xing-out all our pride and pretentions, making us Creation's tops.

Yes! Just say yes to life, to truth, to beauty, to peace and to God alone.
Zap hate…and take every thought captive, His heavenly grace will atone.
Then the Alphabet Soup, will be the stars that direct your ship from above,
And you'll walk all of your days, in the warm glow of His undying love.
Therefore, walk humbly before your Lord and learn your ABC's
<u>July 6-7, 2017</u>

The Answer!

The yards were full of signs it seemed.
Some said Bush and Quayle.
The others had signs in their yards, too,
They simply said, *"For Sale."*

"For Sale?" I pondered for many a mile,
I didn't have a clue.
And then it hit me like a jolt,
Their payments were way past due.

They'd lost their jobs, they'd lose their homes,
They'd lose their pants, no doubt.

They'd lose their will to will again,
Rain wasn't the only drought.

I drove my Chevy with no reverse,
To get my welfare check.
Me and my car were a lot alike,
Both a totally worthless wreck!

On the way home, I saw a man,
An aroma of so much sorrow.
A bent and broken, homeless man,
A taste of my tomorrow?

I fell on my knees and cried *"Dear God!"*
"I cannot take much more."
He said, "The answer is very clear, my son,
Just vote for Clinton and Gore."
Written in El Dorado Hills California in 1992

The Least of These!
(Matthew 25:34-46)

When I was a kid, we had poor folks all over this land.
Didn't give it much thought. We'd give a helping hand.
Hobos, bums, riffraff and sundry kinds of other malaise.
But, no problem, *"You have the poor with you always."*

So you see, our helping hands were only extended so far.
We'd pray for 'em saying, *"Hitch your wagon to a star."*
And that was well and good, but I must quickly confess,
Intentions made them never less nor more...homeless.

When the roll is called, wherever it's going to be called,
Who among us will simply stand there and be appalled?
We prayed for them and wished them a most fond adieu.
He will then say, *"Depart from me. I never knew **YOU.**"*

That's unfair! Praying for and treating them like a brother,
Told them I had done for them like I'd done for no other.
But lost all hope, knowing I'd just become homeless too.
And, that sad, sad reminder will forever ring long and true,
"Always do for others as you would have them do unto you."
May 10, 2018

The Melody of Love!

It was a day like thousands past,
Blue skies, a wispy random cloud,
That leaves no trace, refusing to last,
But for a while, quiet and not so loud,
And forgotten….a long lost shroud.

When night is dark, the hours are long,
But lyrics of love survive the gloom,
And sing their song. But, what's wrong
With God, refusing to play along,
And a rose, declining to bloom?

Neither poets nor I can tell,
'Tis true, what God or clouds will do,
To end the game. First born Adam fell,
And ended up beyond the pale,
While changing all we thought we knew.

Love has no beginning, it has no end.
Original sin will abide.
While mysteries refuse to bend,
But ofttimes an ear will lend,
Who set their sin of pride aside.
And
As pure and as white as a dove,
Once again sing,
"The Melody of Love."
July 11, 2017

The Twenty-Minute Fix!

Life is full to the brim, of Kipling's twin evils.
"If" I speak of the poet's *Triumph and Disaster*.
Depression farmers endured their boll weevils,
Di Vinci, his bad lighting and cheap plaster.

The terrible *Tell-Tale Heart* did Poe no favors,
Nor ultimately did Frost's *Road Less Traveled*.
Neanderthal man's glyphics, in old one-cavers,
Made sophisticated France come unraveled.

Hitler's *Third Reich*, a one-thousand-year reign,
Was about nine-hundred and ninety years short.
Alexander the Great conquered the world in vain,
While NASA, even in triumph, often had to abort.

Dr. Jonas Salk triumphed like very few before,
But cancer, man's scourge, still looks for a cure.
And bad kings and worse rulers tend to ignore,
Every child of God who chooses life to endure.

So, it's quite clear to me, as I ponder these two,
Triumph is often simply disaster gone awry,
And *Disaster* can be a winner from out of the blue,
When this simple formula, we test and apply.
I can do all things through Christ who strengthens me.
Philippians 4:13
April 24, 201

Time to Pay the Bill!

The time just simply stood still,
On old Cypress Ridge Hill,
And in the Texas *"Ville."*

It was His perfect will,
Ink without a quill,
Presidential Seal!
Pay the bill!
It's real.
September 11, 2020
See A Bell Without a Clapper!

Truth Is!

Tis true that Truth is not always funny,
But it's the only thing that will set us free.
Free to laugh and free to cry,
Free to say hello, and free to say goodbye...
Oftentimes bringing a tear to one's eye.
Perhaps we'll understand it better,
In that sweet, by and by.
Inspired by my Sis, Lanora
And
John 14:6
October 13, 2020,

Turn Around and Dance!

She smiled at me and said, *"Before you decide,*
Please put away some of that dumb Texas pride,
You might want to look at it from every side."
Naturally I said, *"Sweetheart, I have no regret."*
That's when she broke down and literally cried,
Then I sweetly suggested, *"Just do a pirouette."*
She blurted, *"What are you talking about?"*
I kindly replied, *"I want to see you inside out!*
Can you twist and shout?"
Revised December 9, 2019

Twenty Ways to the Happy Life???
(In response by a list of things by the same title)

If you wanna be happy, wear the best and prettiest shoes,
While the other five "You's" world-wide, give you the blues.
And so, if you just sit on your butt eleven hours every day,
And sleep without a pillow, well, you've got the devil to pay.

I hear you talking. My dad was tall and I was short and fat,
And I'll be able to resist women, food, danger, and all that.
And if I shake my head real hard, my limbs will come to life.
And if I chew all my food on the right, that will end all strife.

Tea bags in my stinking tennis shoes, takes me back to # one,
And going without sleep eleven hours a day, well, I'd be done.
If I'm not mistaken, Einstein is right. In four years I'd unfurl.
Even if I ate all the red, green and gold apples in the world,

Which comes first the chicken or the egg, health or laughing?
And Wikipedia wanting to cut your life in two by just halving?
And being lazy and inactive might kill you quicker'n smoking,
A ten-watt light bulb's got nothing to do with it! You're joking?

When taking a bath, my body temp won't heat the water one bit.
But could eat razor blades when stomach acid is pitching a fit.
And, about that ovum being big'ern a sperm by a country mile?
No thank you. I'll just keep on living with a big ole Texas smile!
March 7, 2018 in Fort Bragg

When Hurting Becomes Healing!

That life has brought me to this point cannot be denied.
Eternity longs for insights and hopes that one is justified.
Nor would I attempt to ignore even one careless thought.
But sadly, life is spent, and the proverbial farm is bought.

Taking the road most written about, the narrow one indeed.
Abundance escaped me, putting the harvest before the seed,
Wondering what was missing, so much yet to ponder, to see.
And waiting upon the Lord who had promised to set me free.

Light survives after the star dies, like *"found"* follows *"lost."*
And leaves one a broken spirit, because leaving exacts its cost.
If the pain ever leaves at all, it goes most grudgingly slow,
Quite often despite the words, *"We go high, they go low."*

Now I must answer the question: *Where has life brought me?*
Why all the freedom that I'd dreamed about was not at all free.
What good does it do, when wretched loneliness abounds?
When the dreamer of dreams has made all his wistful rounds?

And, here's what I've learned from a prophetic word a few years ago.
I've learned the most important thing that life teaches us to know,
He said I'd find myself alone and living life in my appointed hell.
He was right of course, and perhaps the pain will never cease.
I've learned that the love of Christ is a love that will never fail.
And in the learning, if not always in life, I find sweet peace.
April 26, 2018

When I say I'm a Christian!

When I say I'm a Christian,
It means I'm a follower of Jesus Christ.
And that my redemption has been priced.
That He paid it all for me,
On a star-crossed tree.
It's not a political statement,
It's a sin abatement.
It has nothing to do with tearing our country apart;
It has everything to do with changing my heart..
And on those occasion when life goes off the rails,
Just remember there's one thing which never fails,

Because in the end,
Love always prevails.
<u>April 20, 2021</u>

<u>*When Love Trumps Hate!*</u>

What do our souls experience when evil comes,
And now is acceptable simply because it numbs?
Where do we turn, now that our skies are dark,
And evil alone is standing stark?

Is there a hope beyond the gloom of each new day,
Or is the dark night of the soul here forever to stay?
Is there a course we navigate to overcome the gloom,
Where even in the dessert, love finds a rose in bloom?
Yes, there is reason for hope!
Within everyone's hear- hope lives in a diversity of songs,
<u>Where love prevails and is given first place where it belongs.</u>

<u>*Without a Song!*</u>

And so life goes on, but I cannot imagine how, without a song.
Life wouldn't be worth the going on, without a song.
Every dog has his bone, but, truth be known,
I'd never make it without a song!
And a sweet song in my heart,
Is a good place to start,
If I'm to be a part of,
The human race.
So please give,
Me some,
Space,
For,
My Song. And, if I must,
I'll sing my song alone,
Until I find that elusive land,

Called,
Home Sweet Home.
March 6, 2021

Yesterday's Wine!

Love songs and roses entwine,
As I ponder yesterday's wine.
When life was high,
Love was wishing,
And all the while,
I went fishing!
April 8, 2020

We end the penultimate chapter with a few thoughts provoked by my rereading and pondering what I've written! First, don't go fishing if your marriage is on the rocks. Not if you care about saving it, that is. Now that's a metaphor for men. Ladies, you can use your own imagination to say pretty much the same thing with a like metaphor. One suggestion might be, *"Don't go shopping"* if your marriage is falling apart for overspending your combined incomes!

Other tips? Don't forget the importance of music on and in your marriage. If, in the beginning, you had an *"Our Song,"* remember it and return to that phase of a good marriage. Are those memories precious enough to destroy? If they are, then you should consider counselling to save the marriage…and those memories. If they are not, then likely you should seek an amicable parting of the ways. But think first of what made it your song? Those causes produce strange effects in a marriage if it was ever good at all.

But ultimately, thank the Lord for what you had…then face the world with a tear, but with a tip from Kris Kristofferson, Thank the Lord, For *The Good Times!* (sung best by Ray Price)! And that's not an opinion, that's a fact!

Then simply do your best at, as St. Paul suggested, *Forgetting the past and pressing on to the mark of the high calling of God in Jesus Christ!*

P.S. Should anyone find that anything I've had to say in any of these 337 poems which has helped you, please send me an email and tell me about it. I would consider that a blessing. My email address is the very last thing I've written on the last page of this book. Page 262.

● ● ●*Love's Ellipsis*● ● ●

A sketch by Maria Hoffman, given to me by Maria, a partner in prayer and my next-door neighbor, along with Peter, her husband. Where there is no pain, there is no gain! Maria went to be with our Lord on September, 3, 2021. Her eternal abode is now in heaven with our Lord. But her memory will live through all eternity. She gained everything God had to offer…in, and through, Jesus Christ! One must *die in* Christ, if one hopes to be raised *with Christ!*

CHAPTER 13
Poems about,

WISDOM

A Family Tradition!

A blowing wind and a restless heart,
Never quite knowing where to start.
Just searching for any place to land.
Needing someone to hold my hand.

So I'll just keep on doing it my way,
Surely it must be in my family DNA.
A soul that's aching, not finding rest.
So why not go on and give it my best.

It's our time-honored family tradition,
Teardrops fall with each new condition.
Every succeeding generation moves it.
Each new novel thing I seek, proves it.

But, the journey will destroy my spirit,
The glitter will fade as I come nearer it,
Still leaving me with aught than I had.
Every choice goes from bitter to bad.

Will I awaken and consider my choice,
Returning to where I met my first loss?
And hear again that still small voice,
"Come home by the way of the cross."
Dedicated to Maria Hoffman…
May 7, 2018

All Things Considered!

Who then amongst us is <u>wise</u>,
And knows all there is to know?
Is heaven but hope in disguise?
And water just unfrozen snow?
I need more than, yes*!* or *no*!

And what <u>is</u> a *catcher in the rye?*
How fast do slow boats to China go?
Can we measure how high the sky?
Is there wind, if it doesn't blow?
The angels don't even know!

Wisdom? Just a concept? Or is it real?
Maybe wisdom resides in the heart;
Or, perhaps it is something we feel?
There must be somewhere to start.
Perhaps only God can impart!

It's neither the sellers nor the bidders,
But I think I know who sealed the deal.
The truly wise is she who considers,
The lilies of the field!
<u>April 24, 2019</u>

<u>A Small Dent in Heaven!</u>

This world would have been mostly, just about the same,
Had I never been born, nor had I ever entered the game.
For I gave so very little of myself, to either friend or foe,
And, what little I did give, few if any, will ever know.

I invested my time in education, and on diplomas and degrees,
Determined to distinguish myself, like the forest from the trees.
But it's long been claimed, *<u>"Faith can make mountains move."</u>*
Why had I not exercised my faith? I had so very much to prove.

Emptying my heart and my head, convincing everyone...of what?
Of all the foolish flotsam and jetsam, which I so soon forgot?
Perhaps I was trying to convince myself, of my wonderful worth?
For I thought, just as my Creator, I could move heaven and earth!

So, you see, my life's been a waste of time, both God's and mine.
The plumpest, sweetest grapes I took, leaving the others...the vine.
Now, I look back over the many years, and bow my head to pray,
And my Lord quietly appears and asks, *"What have you to say?"*

When standing face-to-face with Truth, one becomes a winner,
As plaintively one cries out, *"Lord, have mercy on me a sinner."*
And it was, a special moment in time, in the twinkling of an eye.
I would be singing His praises forever, in that sweet by and by.

There's not a lot can be said of a man, when it takes so little time,
To write it all down and make a record...in a simple little rhyme.
But if the poet is true, honest and faithful, and is sorry for his sin,
Perhaps if others will reflect on his words, they too may come in.
Now back to my original confession, back where these verses began,
Again I will confess. I gave a little bit of nothing, for my fellowman,
But I'll make a slight dent in heaven, where I know my Savior waits,
When,
Joyfully He'll be swinging wide, those *"Welcome Home"* Pearly Gates!
July 17, 2017

A Trio's Trials!

Daniel's lions were immense,
But Balaam's ass had common sense.
Jonah was quite simply dense.
All pressed their cause.
Was recompense,
Without Laws!

Blessed Assurance!

We have been trained from a very tender age, to purchase insurance,
Home, life, and auto, just to name a few; and, it only cost a pittance.
Well, that's what the brokers say. It's not their money; so, why care?
We work two or three jobs. To live without insurance, we don't dare!

Everyone agrees, insurance is critical; and, inarguably, it must be had.
Counting the cost is dangerous, it's neither an option, nor a passing fad.
Those that have it don't need it; but, those without it won't take heed.
Neither hell nor high water will bring help, the world thrives on greed.

Now this sad karma, has brought the poet to his original point of view,
He thus declares, there's another premium, which will one day come due.
Tragically there was a terrible price to pay …on a hill called, *"The Skull,"*
By an itinerant preacher, crucified for the world; thus, making Death null.

He wasn't purchasing insurance, but paying a ransom for you and for me.
Bringing abundant life, the blessing of liberty, and what it means to be free.
Purchasing an eternal premium, for there is no such thing as cheap grace.
In agony on that old rugged cross, he took yours…and he took my place.

He once said, "For God so loved the world, that He gave His only Son,
That whosoever believed in Him would not perish when this life is done.[1]
The Most Holy Father, who spoke the stars and the planets into being,
Proclaimed that eternal life was in Jesus Christ, by faith, not by seeing.

So, you say, *"I'll believe it when I see it."* To which I respond, *"No,
You'll see it when you believe it."* For faith is the only way to go.[2]

He stands at your door and knocks. He wants you to invite Him in.[3]
He's ready, He's willing, He's able to cleanse you from all your sin.
When you've done everything you can think of to be saved, to be born again,
You will hopefully throw up your hands and shout, *"I give up! I can't win!"*
He will softly and tenderly whisper to you, *"That's all I've been waiting for,
You <u>can't</u> do it yourself, it has already been done. My Son has won the war."*

And with His great salvation, He throws in the very first, *"Second Blessing."*
Blessed Assurance, It comes instantly with salvation, like salad with dressing.
St. Peter says, <u>we are kept by the power of God</u>, through faith unto salvation.[4]
You mean I don't have to keep my salvation? That's a heartwarming revelation!

St. Paul says, *"I know whom I have believed and am persuaded <u>that He is able</u> <u>To keep</u> what I've committed unto Him, against that day.*[5] It graces my new label,
People tell me quite frequently, *"I don't think I can keep my new salvation."*
"I know you can't! But, He has promised to keep it for you."[6] *An eternal vacation!"*
John declared, *"And this is the promise that he has promised us, even eternal life."*[7]
If you've been truly born again, His Spirit will wash away, all your struggle and strife.
For God keeps not only us, He also keeps His promises, His essence is sacrificial love;
And, when He sent His only son to purchase our soul, heaven came down from above.[8]

"We can know, that we know," John said, *"If we believe that this life is in the Son."*[9]
His Amazing Grace and Blessed Assurance, can never be lost, it's simply *"one and done!"*
So when you hear Jesus calling for you to accept His saving grace, to come and dine,[10]
The angels will shout with us through the ages, *"Blessed Assurance, Jesus is mine!*
O what a foretaste of glory divine."
Forever and forever! Amen!
<u>July 25th, 2017,</u>

<u>Footnotes:</u>
1. John 3:16;
2. Ephesians 2:8-9;
3. Revelation 3:20;
4. I Peter 1:5;
5. II Timothy 1:12;
6. See F.N. 4 & 5;
7. I John 2:25;
8. See F.N. 1;
9. I John 5:13;
10. See F.N. 3
KJV

Death's Final Chime!

Life's just pennies on the dime,
Somewhat like a lost *stitch-in-time*,
Seldom sublime.
The door will close.
Death's knell will chime,
As life goes.
May 2, 2018

Divine Call!

Preaching is my divine call.
Can do no other lest I fall.
And much like Paul,
And the Damascus Road,
Through it all,
I abode!

"Embrace Life!"

For the past 25 years I've been fighting the aging Process like two dogs fighting over a bone. I've Done
everything I know to do to beat it, to reverse the process; or, at least to make it stand still. But Without
success. It has slowly dawned on me that the last of life, like the first, is a precious gift from God
So why not take it, embrace it, and chase it… to its very end? For you see,
the end marks the beginning of life without end. Eternity!
So take it! It's yours. You've not earned it, nor have you made it possible. It
is quite simply life's most Amazing and precious gift….life itself.
Embrace it! And do so with all your heart, body and soul. It is the only
life you can ever have, and It can only be accepted as a gift.
And
Chase it! It is your pot of gold at the end of the Rainbow. Full of
beauty, grace and love, a treasure Like no other.
Then finally, you will have found ….eternal youth.
June 4, 2015

Holiness!

My daughter challenged me to write a poem on holiness!
Many folks think the only barometer is to wear a long face.
For starters I can say it is neither that, nor Holy Roller-ness!
I'd call those two *time-honored* ways, a lark and a disgrace.

But a caveat: To be holy is not an easy attribute to define.
From righteousness to withdrawing and becoming a monk.
No! Both of those would include a willingness to resign,
That has as much to do with holiness…as a dead skunk!

Holiness cannot be defined…without starting with God!
Just as wisdom cannot be gained with a course *on-line!*
To humbly bow before His *"Otherness"* might be odd.
But it's the best I can do with this *pea-brain* of mine!
Therefore,
If you desire to be Holy, you must your will *re-align.*
As you stand amazed in His presence!
And for that…you need not wait in line.
Don Claybrook, Sr. Feb. 2, 2022 at Jack's request.

Reflections On Holiness!

She wanted to replace happiness with holiness,
That was indeed her 2022 New Year's resolution.
Will she find Nirvana; or, perhaps a hole abyss?
Achieving her goal with an unachievable solution;
Or perhaps, a deadly pollution?
I hope and pray she achieves such a noble goal,
Her head and heart are surely in the right place,
A goal so commendable, and that, by *ten-fold.*
But has she forgotten? HE put a smile on her face?
Called Amazing Grace!
Which begs the question: How does holiness work?

Does one get it by retreating to his own *Waldon Pond?*
Or by turning to the Holy Father hoping for a perk:?
Or being zapped by Merlin's Wand!
Or some fantasy beyond?
Our Lord left his Father and all of heaven's glory,
So that we might have the abundant life on earth!
Love is the theme of the world's greatest story,
When LOVE became a person, in a manger at birth,
Giving us supreme worth!
So, it would seem that perfect holiness is out of reach.
We can only hope to *approach it* as we play the game!
For between holiness and happiness there is no breach!
We chose *the good fight* in which there is no shame,
Where Holiness and Happiness,
Are one and the same!
February 10, 2022

My Happiness Depends on Holiness!

A person in Christ, should be able to sing their songs!
Happiness and Holiness are mutually inclusive.
Singing one without the other, turns rights to wrongs!
Creating a large void, if we're not willingly intrusive.

We sing our happiness and holiness to our Lord,
For He loves us, and is a friend, like no other,
We might come unglued, quite unlike The Bard,
But our Lord sticks closer than a brother.
Don Claybrook, Sr. June 20, 2022.

Hurting!

The end comes and pain dies slow!
And leaving's but one way to go.
We reap and sow,

Our last alert,
And now we know
<u>Awful hurt.</u>

I Ran The Race!

Hitched my wagon to a star.
My Lord was with me near and far,
No hero nor,
King for a day
Far under par,
But,
<u>I DID play!</u>

Jesus Christ is Lord!

I enjoy writing poetry, I do it for various reasons, but mostly just for fun.
I write poems for birthdays, for special days, for simply getting it done.
I've written poems for my daughters. Written for any old wind that blew.
I've done poems of yesterday, today and tomorrow, I've written quite a few.

Now, I ponder and prepare to write more verse, and explore the possibility,
What can I write, nor vain nor trite, neither *"maybe"* nor *"what <u>might</u> be?"*
As I reflect upon what is, or what might have been, I'm visited by a Friend,
The Spirit softly breathes to me, *"Write about The Beginning and the End."*

That was just enough to convince me, when I write of the people I love,
I had forgotten the most important One, the One who came from above.
I frequently tell Him how much I love Him, because He first loved me,
But, I'd never written a poem to share with Him, all in a brand-new key.

Carefree as a boy and his dog, on a summer's day. I, only twelve years old.
Just as lost as the pearl of the woman; or, the Prodigal who had left the fold.
All the world had to offer, tugged at my heart; but I couldn't sleep at night.
Miserable as the man who built more barns. Something just wasn't right.

Oh, I had read that God so loved the world that He sent His only Son,
That He was the Way, The Truth and the Life, e'er even time had begun.
But my sins, my doubts, my questions…had me almost going insane.
And rumor had it, that the road to heaven, was marked by a narrow lane.

Try as I might, I couldn't understand, why Jesus Christ would take <u>my</u> place,
Upon reflection today, I know it's simply because I'm part of the human race!
For it's not God's will that any should perish, but that all should choose Life!
To leave that choice unmade is the same as choosing death, anguish and strife.

I'd tried everything, yet nothing worked. And then I said, *"I just gave up!"*
That's when it happened, when I heard Him say, *"Here, drink from My cup."*
Like a trusting child with a child-like faith, I drank, and my world stood still!
Without knowing…by faith, I'd been set free by the Cross on Calvary's Hill.

I'd been saved! I'd been born-again! I'd tasted new wine, joy without end!
He was now my *Alpha and Omega*, my Lord, my Savior, my *"Forever Friend!"*
I love you Lord Jesus, come abide with me. I'm so thankful for what you did,
You carried away my sin. I could never repay. There was no *quid-pro-quid*.

And now when my heart is broken, and when my life is ripped apart,
I just give it all to Him, who heals me and gives me a brand-new start.
Placing it all in his nail-scarred hands…not thinking of reason nor rhyme,
He faithfully makes me whole again, through His healing hands of time.

God was in Christ, reconciling the world to Himself…because He loved us so.
I want so much to tell Him how thankful I am, that He refused to let me go.
I humbly bow and acknowledge Him, as at the cross did the Roman guard,
I will declare throughout the ages and for eternity, that *Jesus Christ is Lord!*

And as St. Paul has so aptly written, in that beautiful Philippian hymn,
He is Lord, He is Lord, He has risen from the grave and He is Lord,
Every knee shall bow, every tongue confess…That Jesus Christ is Lord!
<u>July 5, 2017</u>

Jots and Tittles!

Blessed the man who heeds not,
Every tittle and every jot,
With all he's got.
Ungodly man,
His complete lot,
<u>In God's hand.</u>

Just the Beginning!

Now here's the rest of my story,
My crown is laid up in glory.
Those golden stairs,
And heaven's bliss.
Nothing compares,
To,
Love's sweet kiss!
<u>April 28, 2019</u>

Just Trust!

Well, some say the rain falls on the unjust, as well as on the just!
While others contend that, *"Promises were made to be broken."*
Winter and Spring rains and promises might settle the dust,
And many of our reckless thoughts may be left unspoken.
But till pie crusts and nails turn into crumbs and rust,
And all our promises become more than just a token,
We will go from *The Big Bang* to *The Big Bust,*
Until our better angels are woken,
And in Him, We once again
<u>Trust! And that's not an option! IT'S A MUST!</u>

Keep Rowing!

Of all the sad facts of life,
Filled with much bitterness and strife,
Between husband and wife.
Keep the canoes going,
They cut the water like a knife,
So, keep on rowing!

Kicking The Can!

When you think you can't, you can,
Become a much better man.
Don't kick the can,
Down the road.
Just get up again!
And reload!

Love's Sweet Refrain!
(A poem about pain)

I've learned to turn and walk quietly away,
Although I've gone, a part of me will stay.
When it's time to say my lonely goodbyes,
It makes the leaving harder, as time flies.
Then
Time marches on, as the saying goes,
Sadly, the thorn, never becomes a rose.
But with each new step, the pain will fade.
Are those memories, or a cheap *Charade?*
And we ponder.
Will that deep down hurt ever go away?
No! It remains.
But one thing we know which *will* stay,
Pain cherishes not the return of those times,

But God's love forgives the worst of crimes!
Furthermore,
He uses pain and joy to bring about good!
God's grace makes *ought* become *should,*
Trust! Though you don't know His plan.
For a heartbroken man can stand,
Where few men can,
And still remain,
An honorable,
Man!
Written by Don Claybrook, Sr. and my daughter, Liberty Jackson (Jack), via email.
February, 27, 2022

My Search for Eternity!
(On turning *forty-seven*)

My forty-sixth year was spent looking for eternity.
I searched in the most unlikely places…
A Kansas City Convention Center;
A hospital which became a mental ward;
I even searched Hell.
No eternity here, except for the memories,
Not many good.
Two-score and seven? Perhaps only a bridge to *forty-eight*;
Or, maybe just a number in the midst of numbers.
Nothing special. Something to be forgotten.
No eternity here, except for memories,
Not many good.
I looked for eternity on a *stone-covered* hill,
As one was committed to the cold hard earth.
I spoke eternal words that were marked in time.
"Now" was gone forever, to be lost in the past.
No Eternity here, except for the memories,
Not many good.
I looked for eternity in time and space;

But time passed, and space was dark.
And I was alone and afraid.
Afraid because my time and my space were dreadful.
No eternity here, except for the memories,
Not many good.
My memories were shrouded in mystery.
I looked for a glimmering glow of light,
Anything that would keep hope alive.
When all hope is gone, the void becomes
A hurting place.
In my absolute desolation of spirit and mind,
I turned to *The Other* who was beckoning me home.
That was it! I just wanted to go home,
To the bosom of warmth, and life and love,
To be there again; or, perhaps for the very first time.

I would return to hearth and home,
To the arms of mercy and abundant grace.
And that's when I knew.
When I knew the darkness,
In the midst of the light.
Sadly, I didn't know where home was.
Could it be that I had never been there?
Perhaps!
My search for eternity was a search for home.
Therefore, I can infer from my ponderings,
This:
Heaven is the eternal search for home!
February 1, 1985
Revised 32 years later, on Dec. 1, 2017,
Because I lost the last four stanzas somewhere along the way.

Not Your Father's "Go-To-God!"

Time was, when we had problems, we turned to God.
But the time would come, we'd hardly give Him a nod,
Knowing we couldn't count on Congress or Uncle Sam.
We decided to just tell our Uncle, "Now, Sam...I am."

And so we were. We could do all things through Christ,
Because the ransom had been paid and the sin excised.
Because He had promised to strengthen us for the road,
We said, *"Yes,"* and in that love, made our eternal abode.

But in time, we slowly came to depend on just, well...us,
Falling from grace recalling, God is a God who is jealous.
Leaning on our own understanding! What we deemed good,
He demanded obedience in determining where we stood.

So, here's where we are: Turning to fate's sad double-S.
By so doing, we've gotten ourselves into one big mess,
Going to that which tires us and makes awfully weary.
By staking our lives on Double-S: Serendipity and Siri.

Time to humble ourselves and pray and confess our sins.
When all is said and done, a win/win means nobody wins.
So, although Serendipity is nice, and Siri helps us much,
God in Christ is always. Not just, *"god in the clutch."*
May 21, 2018

Politics!

Will Rodgers said awhile back,
Some truth is not about white and black!
Lies can talk smack!
So,
In that sad mix,
A bunch of hacks,
<u>Politics!</u>

Prayer!

Father, I'm mostly lost in time;
Just a speck of dust that floats.
I'm neither a reason nor a rhyme,
Nor a child on which a mother dotes.

What is man that thou art mindful of him?
You, who hung the stars and the moon.
Was I no more than a careless whim?
Something to do from morning 'till noon?

I contemplate, but dare not tarry;
I stop my doings but find no rest.
And search the skies, but see not nary
Haven nor anchor, but waves to crest.

I do not see my lot improving,
As reflection's tolls increase.
But in the Spirit's freedom moving,
I lose my soul; there is no cease.

Lose it in You, lose it in Love,
Lose it and just forget to care;
Except for thoughts on things above,
Of angelic wings of a heavenly dove,
Then,
I recall the meaning of prayer.
1995-96 sometime around the birth of Liberty Jackson

The following poem is a prime example of my conviction that there is often very little difference between the Ridiculous and the Sublime; or, in this case, Wisdom. I had a choice as to where I categorized this poem in the 13 categories I included in this collection. My choice could have been The Ridiculous; but, I chose Wisdom because of <u>Love's Ellipsis</u>...*The Way to Wisdom*...three little dots that make all the difference.

Promises and Pie Crusts!

Holidays and regular days both have their places,
People and *house-cats* belong to 2 different races!
If time were money, well now, we'd all be rich,
And if scratching was effective, we wouldn't itch!
Or get shingles!
Good deeds and bad deeds, yes, both can be done.
But you can't be a father, absent a daughter or son!
If I prove to be right and you prove to be wrong,
One of us will cry, while the other sings a song!
And I do love to sing!
Now, apples and oranges are both considered fruit.
Tomatoes? Vegetable/Fruit? Now that's a hoot!
If tomatoes are fruit, and not just a vegetable,
Then I like pumpkins! And those ain't edible!
But hogs love 'em!
Love, hate and indifference, live side by side in life.
When a marriage is good, so do a husband and wife!
If a man and a *house-cat* can become good friends,
Why can't mankind unite a world without ends?
Space bends!
Promises and pie crusts both can be broken,
Good words and bad words, both can be spoken!
If I had two wishes I knew would come true,
I'd give one away, and share one with you!
Now,
I'm through! And here's a clue:
When you consider the Lilies,
Once more,
You will find,
That love is patient and kind!
And,
It was always…on His mind!
BTW, He's a friend of mine!

Won't you be His friend too?
February 9, 2022
See also Potpourri of Spring, page 47,
For a different version!

Prosperity or Posterity?

Just name it and claim it. Think and grow rich!
Just one year more than the seven-year itch.
Prosperity is sure to follow, like wet follows rain.
Eight is enough of poverty's anguish and pain.

Thinking of St. Paul, stuck in Rome under house-arrest,
Did he just tarry with the gospel in abeyance to attest?
Wondering if he e'er came back to the land of his birth,
Hob-knobbing with his cohorts, full of merry and mirth?

To ponder at all, is like reliving the life of our posterity,
Knowing in many ways, they were our only prosperity.
While sharing our wealth with those we love best,
Survivors becoming our heirs upon leaving the nest.
Hence, the age-old question still begs to be answered,
Did they all get lucky? Nor labeled "pre-cancer'ed."
Would they be our posterity by sharing our prosperity?
And be satisfied with a life of humbleness and verity?
Always dreaming of life's sweetest love.
Which never fails, and only comes, from heaven above.
April 24, 2018

Rebel Child!

Jesus was a Rebel Child.
He stayed behind at the Temple.
He made his parents awfully tired,
And justified the simple.

She was caught in the very act,
Her sin was doubly bad!
When the Rebel Child pronounced her clean,
They knew that _they'd_ been had.

"Throw you rocks at her," He said,
As he heard them rant and hiss.
_"That's is, if you <u>are</u> perfectly straight,
And never the mark <u>you</u> miss!"_

He wasn't speaking of their aim,
T'was the last thing on his mind.
He was amazed at what they'd _"seen,"_
Given the fact that <u>they</u> were blind.

_"Why were you there in that place,
Where she worked her trade by night?
If you had been out doing good,
You might have received <u>your</u> sight!"_

So one by one they slinked away,
Their manner meek and mild.
The only one who could've stoned her,
Was the sinless Rebel Child!

And yet his words, they linger still,
"Just go and sin no more."
The one and only Rebel Child,
Refused-----to keep score.

Jesus was a Rebel Child,
He didn't fit their mold.
Yet 2,000 years have proven him,
<u>The greatest story ever told.</u>

Saint or Sinner?
(Luke 15: 11-32)

Once there was a man who had two sons
Who were brought up the very same way.
One of them was his father's favorite,
The other longed for a new kind of day.

To one the world was black and white;
To the other, the sky was blue and gold.
And his rainbow retained all of its hues,
While he quietly left the fold.

He refused to just live out his life,
Doing what *"his people"* had always done.
The other son kept all the family rules,
From daybreak, to the setting of the sun.

Then over in that far removed land,
Where eagles and egos soared,
The sinner cast his lot with others,
And there, his anchor he moored.

After fits and starts, and diver's diseases,
He came to himself and said,
*"I want to go home where my family waits,
While I'm still alive and not dead."*

His father received and welcomed him back,
Where he waited with arms opened wide.
*"Welcome home to the family my son,
And in my love, forever abide."*
The other son couldn't believe the news,
He had stayed at home just to be good.
But the wayward son never lost his place,

In the family…and never would.

So from this eternal story 'tis clear,
That one can, and often does, leave home.
But never loses his place in the family,
In spite of how far he may roam.

And now that wayward son,
(The loser who's now become the winner),
Can drink deeply from the family wine,
And know…the saint is still the sinner.
One saint stayed home,
While the other went out to dinner.
December 8, 2017

Sharon's Rose!

I'll walk the way the wind blows,
And I'll walk The Way that He goes,
The Way He knows!
And it will end,
At Sharon's Rose
With my Friend
May 3, 2018

Sometimes Time!

They say that sometimes, time waits for no man.
But others say that sometimes, time really does!
I know a man who had a *pie-in the-sky-like* plan,
Who could distinguish *what is* from *what was!*

He spread this plan of his any old way he could,
And was patient with those who wouldn't hear.
What is this plan? Why is *what was,* so good,
When *what is,* is still here, with so much fear?

Well, here is your answer…if you really care.
Some <u>two-thousand</u> years ago, Paul said it best!
Yes, there's anger, hate and strife everywhere,
And naught but God's LOVE, Will put it to rest.

Only Love is <u>*what was*</u> and <u>*what is*</u> to be.
For all who recall those hands pierced by nails,
Will be blessed and again and be fully free,
Because <u>*what was*</u> means Love never fails,
And <u>*what is*</u> begins with you!
If we want to be truly free!
But perhaps,
I will agree,
It especially, begins and ends,
with me.
February 7, 2022

Stand Your Ground!

Hourglasses dump their sand,
And move along to *beat-the-band.*
So lend a hand,
When things go wrong.
Take a stand!
You Don't have long.
To,
Sing your song!
May 15, 2019

Summertime in 24 lines!

Where in the world does springtime go?
When the sun decides to give us a show,
When summer demands its place in time,
And brightly comes out, with a heavenly chime.

Summer always infringes, on springtime's song,
But springs fade, they don't last very long.
And they bring to an end the *"Perfect Season."*
But for why? We don't know the reason.

Yes, the seasons fade away, so much like a mist,
And leave this earth knowing, it's truly been kissed.
Away with all our *"Whys,"* and our *"Wherefores,"*
Summer too will pass, in rhythm with all our folklores.

And when this summer's gone, after not so very long,
Might we two just once again, sing *September's Song?*

For the bright colors of autumn, are just as sure to follow,
As Capistrano beckons, to the very last swallow.

And then we will remember, that Nature has its rules,
Just as surely as remembering, that the world has its fools.
That the seasons will come, and with precision will flow,
Perhaps we'll never discern, whence and whither they go,

So, on this beautiful summer night, let's sing our song of life,
And celebrate once again, forsaking all rancor and strife.
And know in our hearts, that heaven's choir, will always sing,
When all God's children, just simply and completely,
<u>Let love rule supreme.</u>
**Written by Liberty and Don…she set the direction
in the first two stanzas. I simply followed. Finished 7/3/17**

TIME STAMP

June 21, 2019 2:34 PM

Wisdom Lives Here!
**Oceanside home Rae and Dean Wisdom,
Photo by Don Claybrook, Sr. on the date shown.**

The ultimate knowledge to be gained from the intellect is but the penultimate as a prelude to wisdom. The penultimate is all that we really ever know through sheer intellect. Any knowing beyond that results in a turning to a divine reconsideration of the lilies of the field. Thus knowledge is both preface and prelude to wisdom. ***Therefore, consider the lilies of the field***…..**Matt. 6:29 KJV**

. . .

Surrender It All!

Blessed the man who heeds not,
Every tittle and every jot,
With all he's got!

Ungodly man,
His complete lot,
In God's hand.
May 3, 2018

The Village of DABDA!

I've been through that village called *DABDA*, Oh, so very many times,
Where dozens of worried folks are *queued up,* in just one too many lines.
I go to The Village for the healing of heartbreak…a kind of death-alert.
My former wife is married again; he an honest lawyer. She? Quite a flirt!
Even As I hurt!
For you to discern what I'm talking about, that is, the *"Initial Treatment,"*
I must explain the letters in *DABDA* before I can make a clear repeatment.
For, every initial in *DABDA's* small village, stands for both good and bad,
Every emotion, each one in that line, when combined, has most likely had.
Keeping the good and tweaking the bad…a tad!
DENIAL, what the D is for, is what everyone does, when tragedy strikes.
Whether a loved-one or a child dies; our *"differences"* become our *"alikes."*
It has long ago been said, *"It takes an entire village, to heal a broken heart,"*
And, it is always certain, we must all rise together; or else, we'll all fall apart.
So, let's make a brand-new start.
ANGER follows denial, just like winter follows autumn; or, day follows night.
When we can no longer deny the facts, we're madder than hell, ready to fight.
But, at whom are we angry? It will not surprise you I guess, we're mad at God!
Most of our days, we have no time at all for Him, won't even give Him a nod.
All Like peas in a pod!
BARGAINING follows anger, when our rage dies, we try hard to make a deal,
With God of course. The One with whom we must bargain, to make our appeal.
"Please Dear God, I never meant for my loved-one to die. Please bring her back,
I'll go to church every Sunday, even some at night, whatever you think I lack."
But, double-dealing God, is not…a valid contract!
DEPRESSION follows denial, anger and bargaining too, as June follows May.
One who's lost everyone, or everything, knows not for whom, nor how to pray.
And there is nothing that affects one like depression does. That's simply a fact.

But things are looking up, help is just around the corner, He has a healing act.
Or else we've all been quacked!
ACCEPTANCE finally arrives, to those who are prepared to spend many days,
Relief never comes instantly, and it never, ever comes, in the same exact ways.
I said I'd been through *DABDA's* Village for many and various reasons.
One step forward, two steps back. Ordering the steps? Different for every season,
When acceptance resonates with reason!
July 22, 2017

They Hadn't a Clue!

Things were good, sky's baby blue.
Weather was perfect, but who knew,
Before day's through…
I'd need a friend
They had no clue
At the end!

Truth Takes Flight!

Without the night, we would lose the stars,
Misplaced, like our *"nears"* and *"fars,"*
A simple gift, neither rhyme nor reason,
More than gray; colors for every season.

Where no color is, there's no light. Life dies.
And without light, there are no *rainbow-skies.*
The norm becomes simply, white and black,
Rainbows won't be the only thing we lack.

Because, when we despair, we let love die.
And death comes with little more than a sigh.
The new color then, is black and white,
With Truth taking…its very last flight.

*

So, where did Veracity, Honesty and Truth go?
This is all I know, a trio of crows took flight!
"One flew east, one flew west, one flew over the coo-coo's nest!"
(With a nod to Ken Kesey)
July 11, 2017, with the last 4 lines added March 27, 2022

What's Your Source?

Well, we have looked at the source;
And yes, we have finished the course,
With no remorse.
We do not hide.
For in that Force,
We abide!
April 8, 2019

While We Slept!

Life's like *one-cent* on a dime,
Ofttimes like a lost *stitch-in-time,*
Seldom sublime.
Then the door closed,
Ringing death's final chime!
And…we dozed.
Date not recorded.

Where Did Tomorrow Go?

Where did tomorrow go?
On which I dreamed my dreams.
Perhaps into thousand yesterdays,
In a thousand forgotten streams.

Where did tomorrow go?
I thought t'would never come.

Like a greeting and a final farewell,
It passed from to…to from.
Where did tomorrow go?
They say, *"It never comes."*
In a heartbeat…gone forever,
Yesterday's distant drums.

Where did tomorrow go?
I search in vain to find.
Loosed and near forgotten,
Like so many ties that bind.

Where did tomorrow go?
With hopes up the sky.
Perhaps I'll never really know,
That *"sweet bye and bye."*

And if there is no tomorrow,
(And I think like the poet does).
How do I posit anything?
Perhaps yesterday never was.

Where did tomorrow go?
Only a fool would say.
I only know in tomorrow's present,
I'll always have today.
<u>Written way back when!</u>

<u>And finally, a word to the wise</u>

● ● ●

Where Wisdom Resides

Do you get your daily news from CNN, Facebook, Fox and Twitter,
Leaving you sadly incoherent, in chaos, and ofttimes bitter?
Don't throw in the towel! Because you're no quitter!`
You might pause briefly, but you must never yield.
Then,
Perhaps you will once again,
Consider,
The Lilies of the field.
The way to wisdom!
August 25, 2019

As we come to the end of this book of poetry, let me do my best to say what true wisdom is. That can best be done with starting by noting what wisdom is NOT. It's not intellect, in the common usage of that word. Wisdom is often found in the most uncommon people…It's a divine gift for a divine purpose. Ultimately, after looking high and low for THE proper definition of wisdom, I've come to this unavoidable realization and conclusion. When we take time to *Consider the Lilies of the Field,* and discover the story they tell, then we will also be discovering what enables all true wisdom!

This brings to an end my collection of poetry. Should you find that anything I've had to say in any of these 337 poems…which has helped you, please send me an email and tell me about it. I would consider it a blessing. My email address is the very last thing I've written in this book, and it's on this…very last page.
Don Claybrook, Sr. Ph.D.
Email: dcowboy@mcn.org

Printed in the United States
by Baker & Taylor Publisher Services